EASY GUITAR
WITH NOTES & TAB

BROADWAY
SONGS FOR GUITAR

ISBN 978-1-5400-5605-4

HAL•LEONARD®

Visit Hal Leonard Online at
www.halleonard.com

Contact us:
Hal Leonard
7777 West Bluemound Road
Milwaukee, WI 53213
Email: info@halleonard.com

In Europe, contact:
Hal Leonard Europe Limited
42 Wigmore Street
Marylebone, London, W1U 2RN
Email: info@halleonardeurope.com

In Australia, contact:
Hal Leonard Australia Pty. Ltd.
4 Lentara Court
Cheltenham, Victoria, 3192 Australia
Email: info@halleonard.com.au

T0087130

STRUM AND PICK PATTERNS

This chart contains the suggested strum and pick patterns that are referred to by number at the beginning of each song in this book. The symbols ⊓ and ∨ in the strum patterns refer to down and up strokes, respectively. The letters in the pick patterns indicate which right-hand fingers play which strings.

p = **thumb**
i = **index finger**
m = **middle finger**
a = **ring finger**

For example; Pick Pattern 2
is played: thumb - index - middle - ring

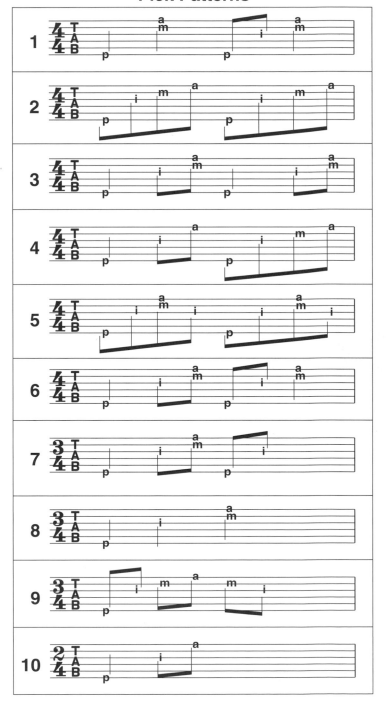

Strum Patterns

Pick Patterns

You can use the 3/4 Strum and Pick Patterns in songs written in compound meter (6/8, 9/8, 12/8, etc.). For example, you can accompany a song in 6/8 by playing the 3/4 pattern twice in each measure. The 4/4 Strum and Pick Patterns can be used for songs written in cut time (¢) by doubling the note time values in the patterns. Each pattern would therefore last two measures in cut time.

All I Ask of You

from THE PHANTOM OF THE OPERA

Music by Andrew Lloyd Webber
Lyrics by Charles Hart
Additional Lyrics by Richard Stilgoe

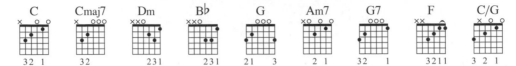

Strum Pattern: 1, 2
Pick Pattern: 2, 4

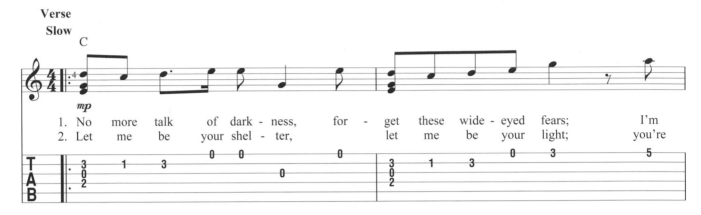

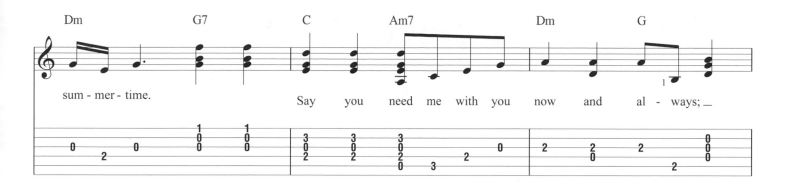

sum - mer - time.　　Say　you　need　me　with　you　now　and　al - ways; —

To Coda ⊕

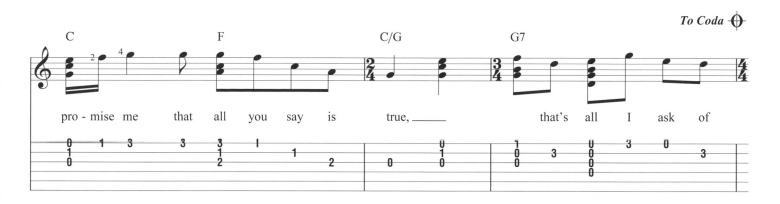

pro - mise　me　that　all　you　say　is　true, _____　that's　all　I　ask　of

|1., 2.

2nd time, D.S. al Coda

⊕ Coda

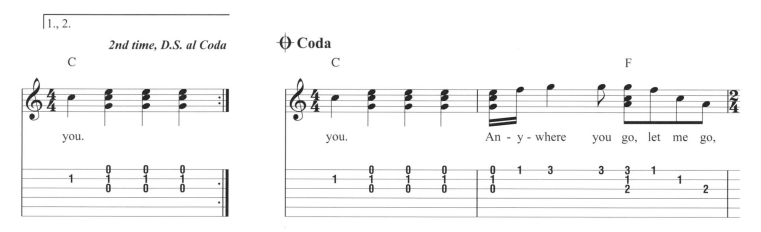

you.

you.　　An - y - where　you　go,　let　me　go,

too; _____　　love　me,　that's　all　I　ask　of　you.

Additional Lyrics

Chorus 2.　Then say you'll share with me one love, one lifetime.
Let me lead you from your solitude.
Say you need me with you, here, beside you.
Anywhere you go, let me go, too.
Christine, that's all I ask of you.

Chorus 3.　Say you'll share with me one love, one lifetime.
Say the word and I will follow you.
Share each day with me, each night, each morning.
Say you love me! You know I do.
Love me, that's all I ask of you.

Any Dream Will Do

from JOSEPH AND THE AMAZING TECHNICOLOR® DREAMCOAT

Music by Andrew Lloyd Webber
Lyrics by Tim Rice

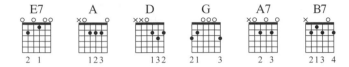

Strum Pattern: 3, 4
Pick Pattern: 3, 4

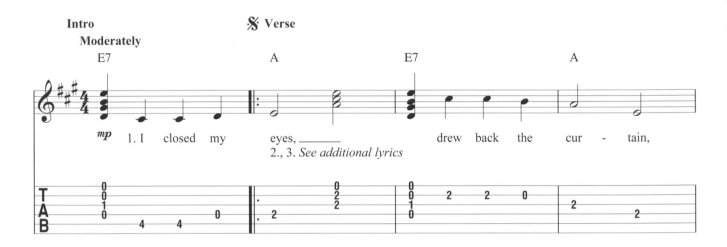

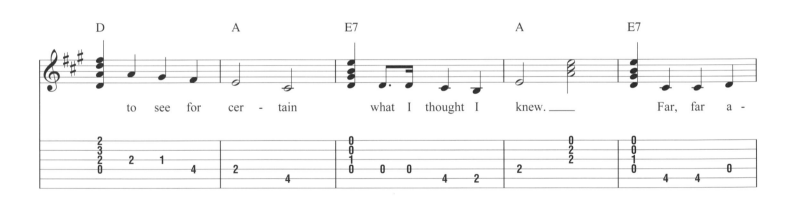

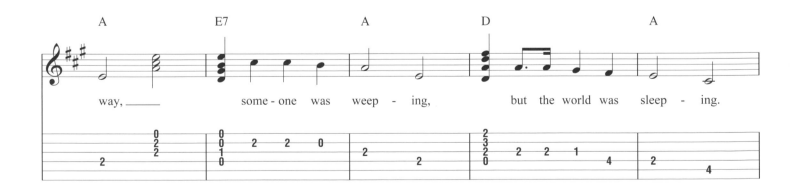

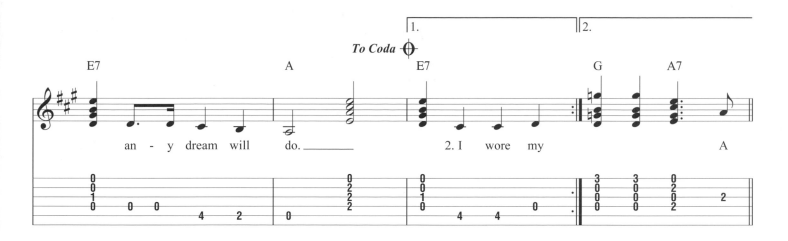

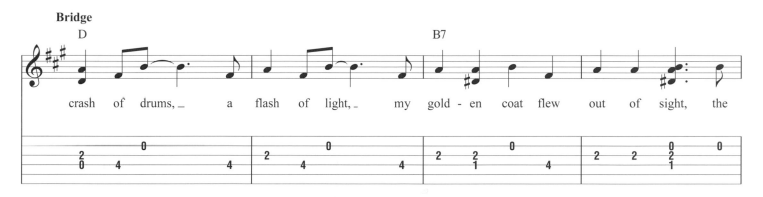

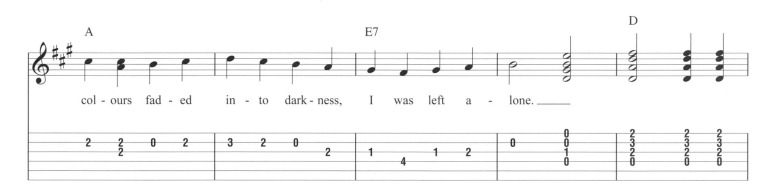

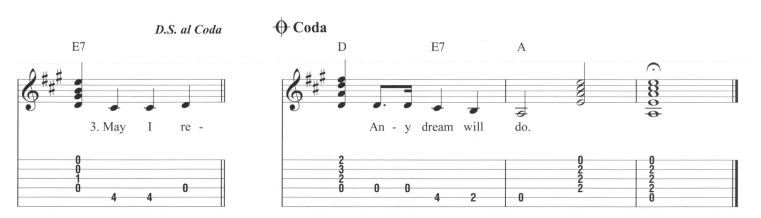

Additional Lyrics

2. I wore my coat with golden lining,
   Bright colours shining, wonderful and new.
   And in the East the dawn was breaking,
   The world was waking. Any dream will do.

3. May I return to the beginning.
   The light is dimming and the dream is, too.
   The world and I, we are still waiting,
   Still hesitating. Any dream will do.

Cabaret

from the Musical CABARET
Words by Fred Ebb
Music by John Kander

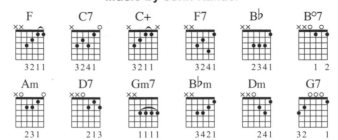

Strum Pattern: 4
Pick Pattern: 5

Verse
Moderately, in 2

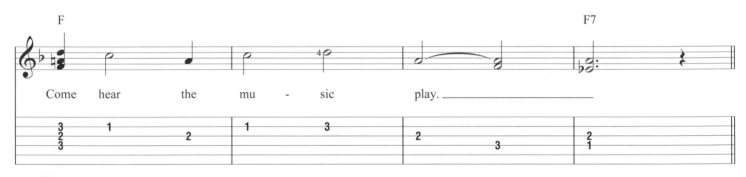

1. What good is sit - ting a - lone in your room? ___
2., 3. See additional lyrics

Come hear the mu - sic play. ___

Chorus

To Coda

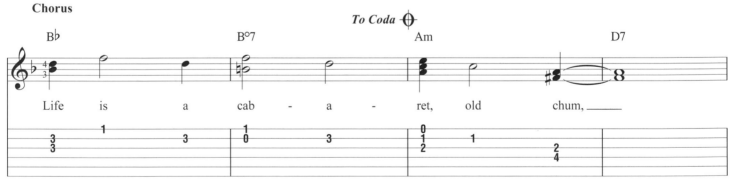

Life is a cab - a - ret, old chum, ___

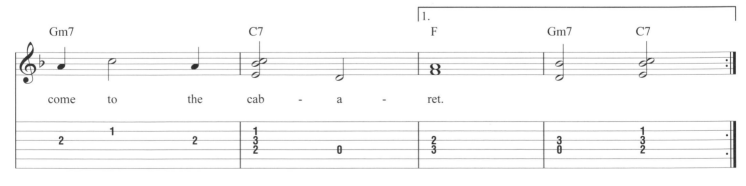

come to the cab - a - ret.

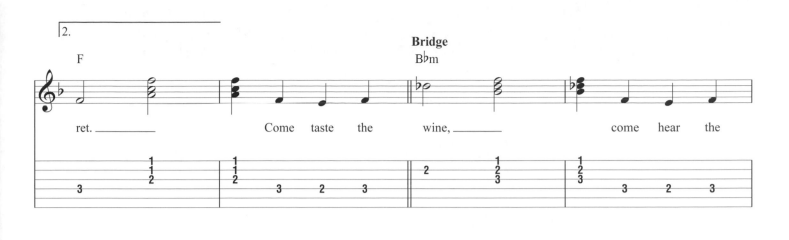

Bridge

ret. _____ Come taste the wine, _____ come hear the

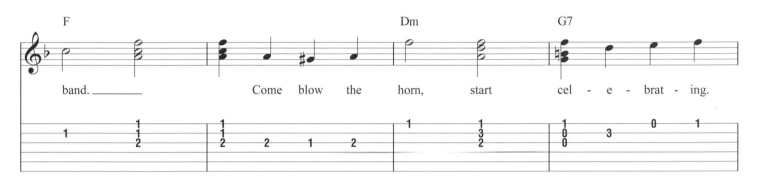

band. _____ Come blow the horn, start cel - e - brat - ing.

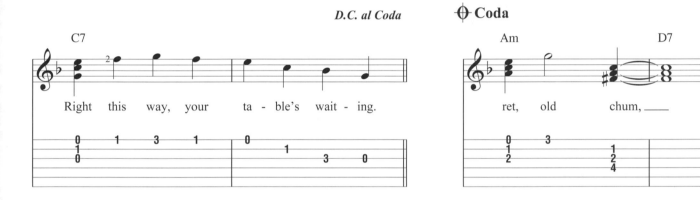

D.C. al Coda   ⨁ **Coda**

Right this way, your ta - ble's wait - ing.   ret, old chum, ___

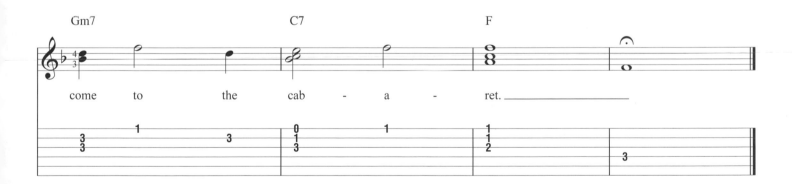

come to the cab - a - ret. _____

Additional Lyrics

2. Put down the knitting, the book and the broom,
   Time for a holiday.

3. No use permitting some prophet of doom
   To wipe ev'ry smile away.

Can You Feel the Love Tonight

from THE LION KING: THE BROADWAY MUSICAL

Music by Elton John
Words by Tim Rice

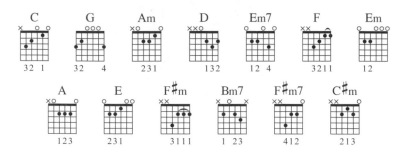

*Tune down 1/2 step:
(low to high) Eb-Ab-Db-Gb-Bb-Eb

Strum Pattern: 1, 6
Pick Pattern: 2, 5

Verse
Freely

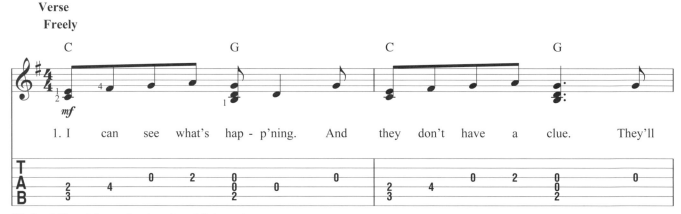

1. I can see what's hap-p'ning. And they don't have a clue. They'll

*Optional: To match recording, tune down 1/2 step.

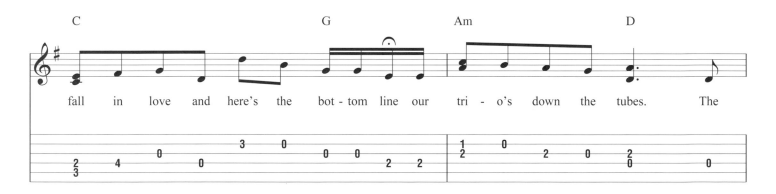

fall in love and here's the bot-tom line our tri-o's down the tubes. The

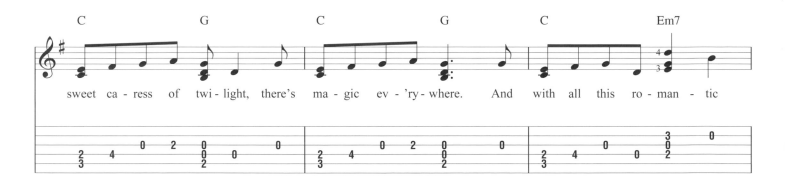

sweet ca-ress of twi-light, there's ma-gic ev-'ry-where. And with all this ro-man-tic

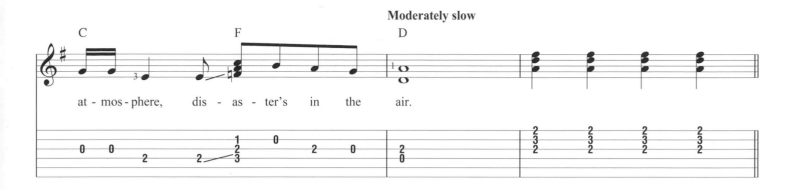

at - mos - phere,   dis - as - ter's   in   the   air.

% Chorus

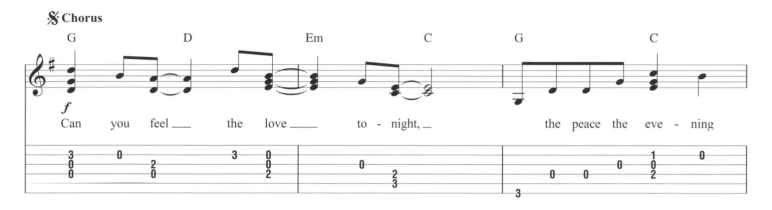

Can   you   feel ___   the   love ___   to - night, ___   the   peace   the   eve - ning

To Coda ⊕

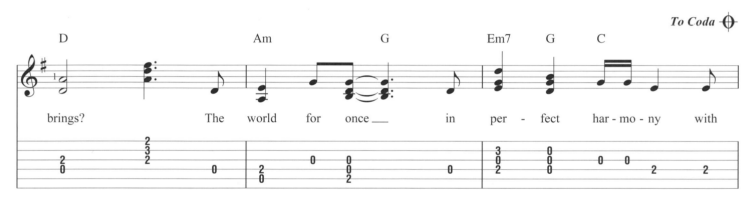

brings?   The   world   for   once ___   in   per - fect   har - mo - ny   with

Verse

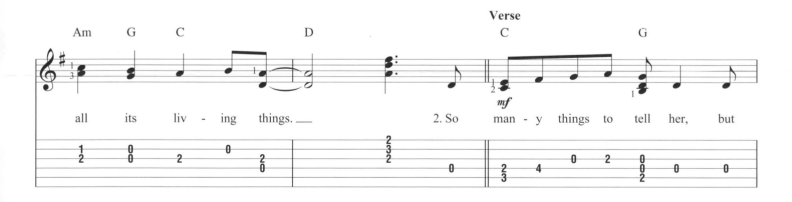

all   its   liv - ing   things. ___   2. So   man - y   things   to   tell   her,   but

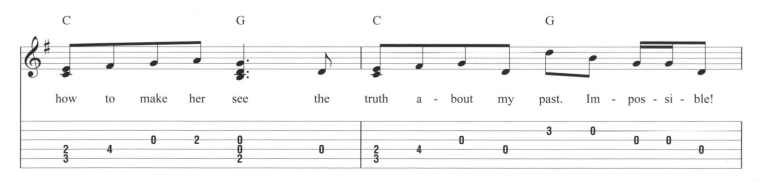

how   to   make   her   see   the   truth   a - bout   my   past.   Im - pos - si - ble!

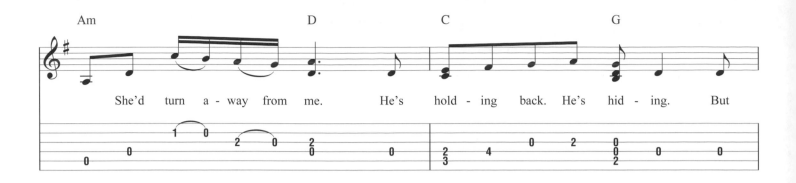

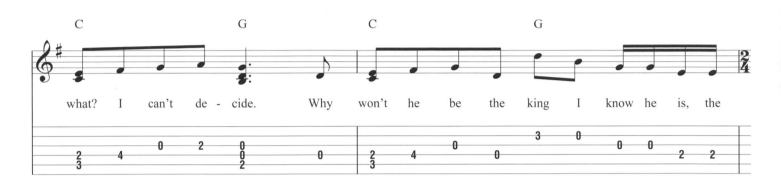

D.S. al Coda

⊕ **Coda**

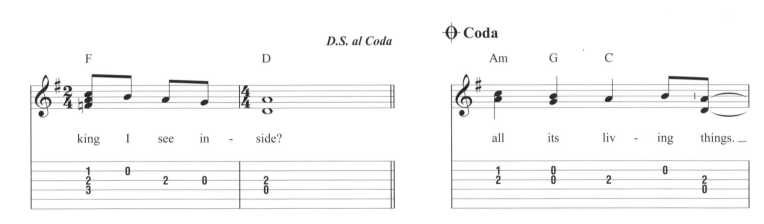

Chorus

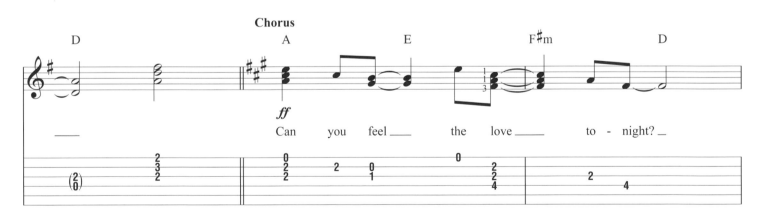

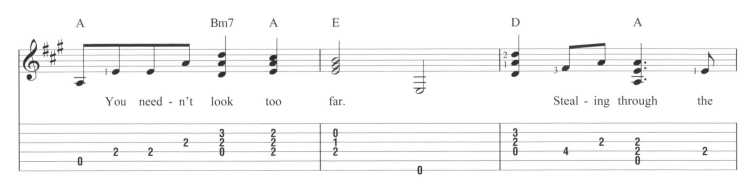

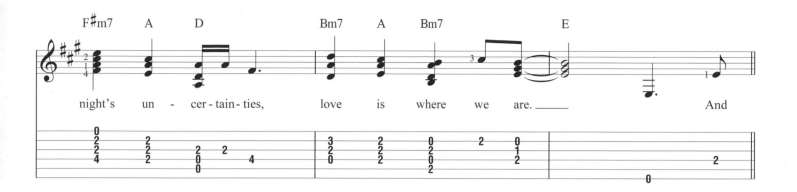

night's un - cer- tain- ties,   love   is   where   we   are. _____   And

Outro

if   he   feels   the   love _____   to - night _____   in   the   way   I

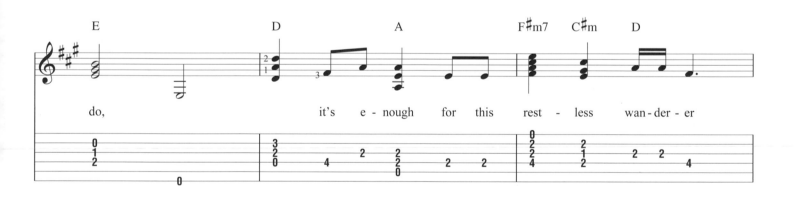

do,   it's   e - nough   for   this   rest - less   wan - der - er

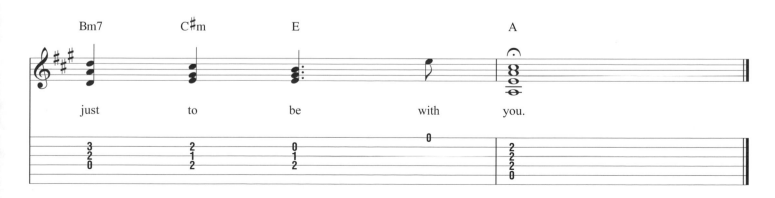

just   to   be   with   you.

Edelweiss

from THE SOUND OF MUSIC

Lyrics by Oscar Hammerstein II
Music by Richard Rodgers

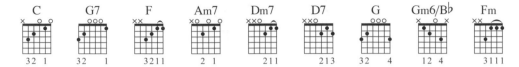

Strum Pattern: 7
Pick Pattern: 7

Slowly

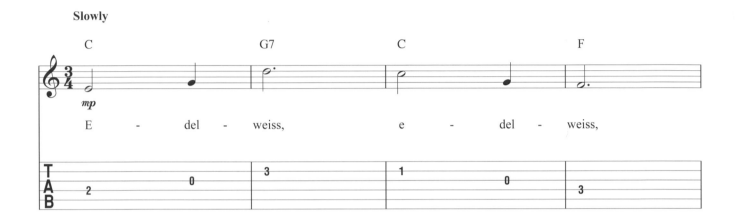

E - del - weiss, e - del - weiss,

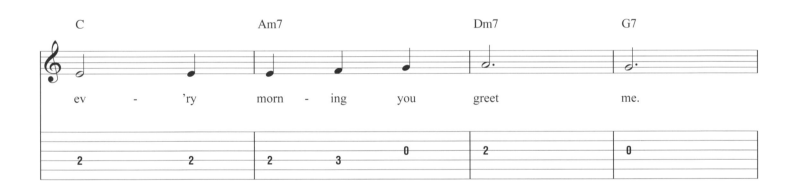

ev - 'ry morn - ing you greet me.

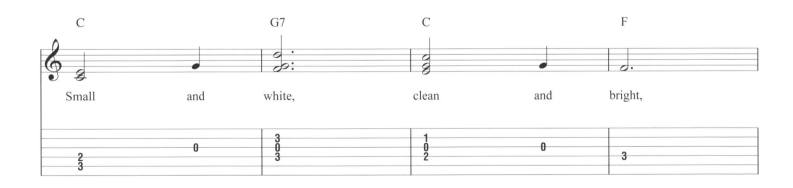

Small and white, clean and bright,

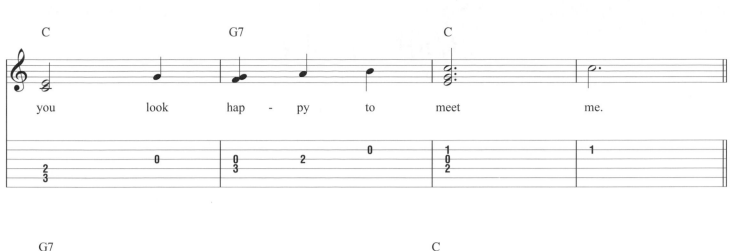

you look hap - py to meet me.

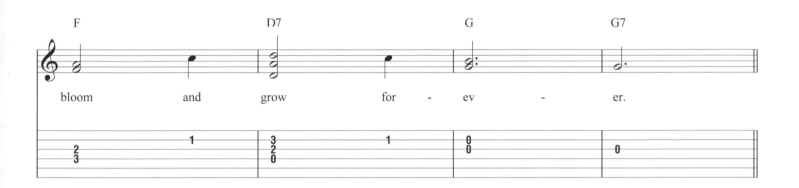

Blos - som of snow, may you bloom and grow,

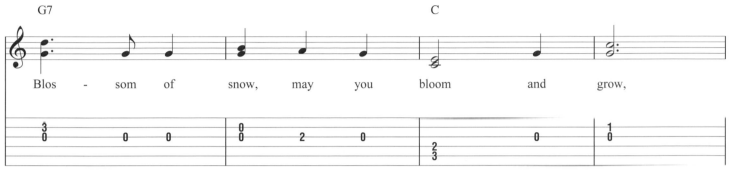

bloom and grow for - ev - er.

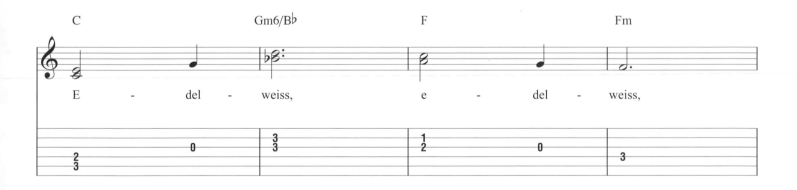

E - del - weiss, e - del - weiss,

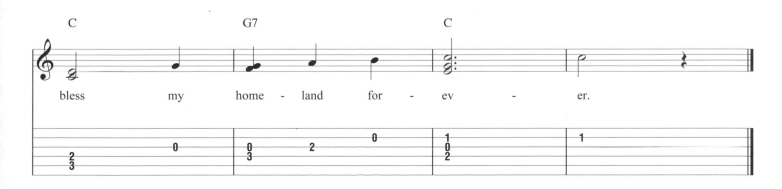

bless my home - land for - ev - er.

Hello, Dolly!

from HELLO, DOLLY!
Music and Lyric by Jerry Herman

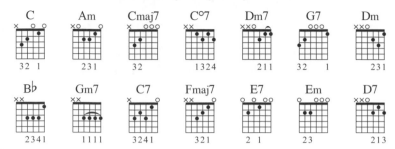

Strum Pattern: 3
Pick Pattern: 3

Verse
Moderately, in 2

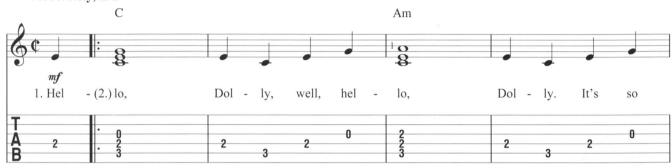

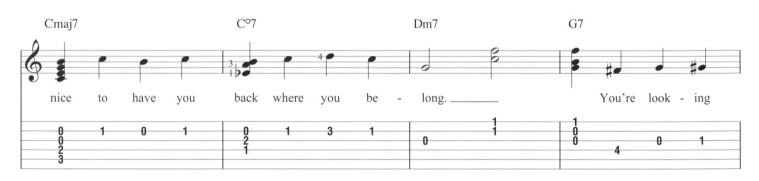

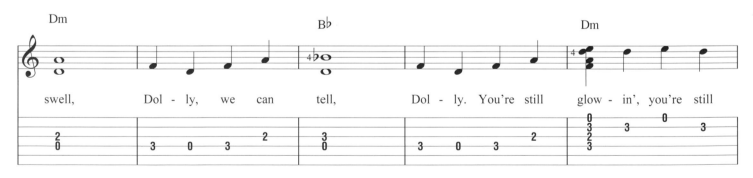

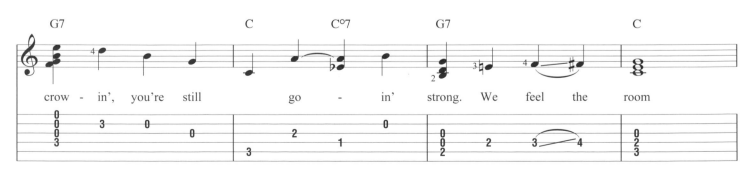

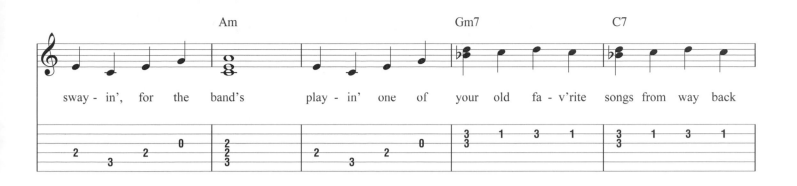

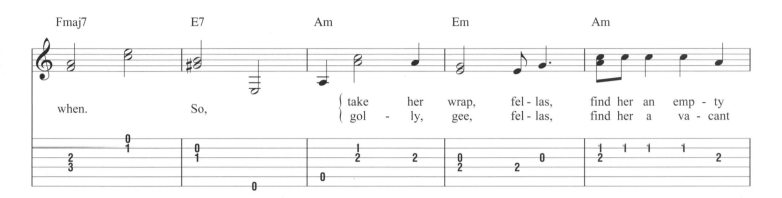

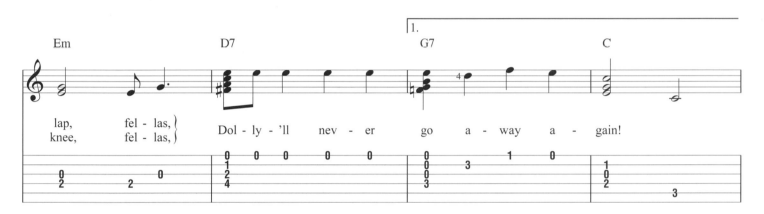

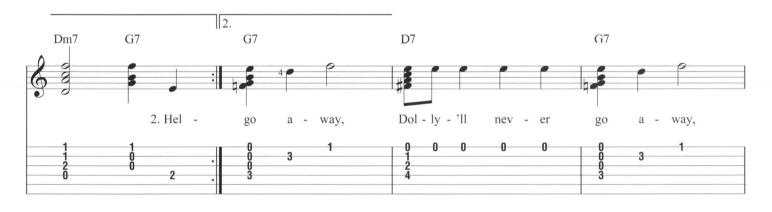

Hey There

from THE PAJAMA GAME
Words and Music by Richard Adler and Jerry Ross

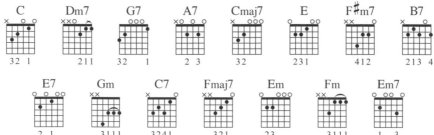

Strum Pattern: 3, 4
Pick Pattern: 3, 5

I Don't Know How to Love Him

from JESUS CHRIST SUPERSTAR
Words by Tim Rice
Music by Andrew Lloyd Webber

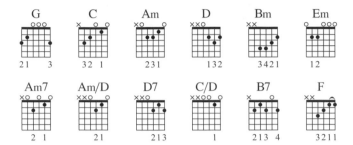

Strum Pattern: 1, 2
Pick Pattern: 2, 4

Intro
Slowly

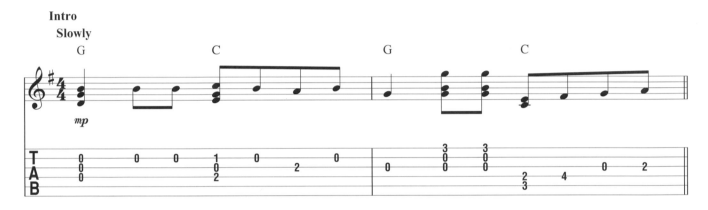

Verse

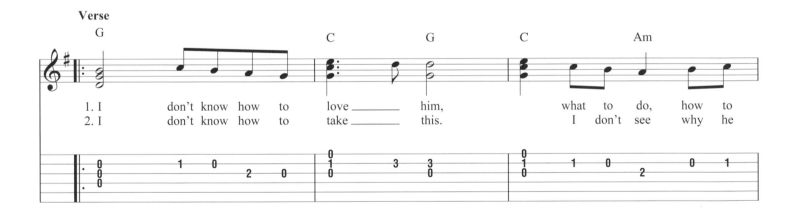

1. I don't know how to love _____ him, what to do, how to
2. I don't know how to take _____ this. I don't see why he

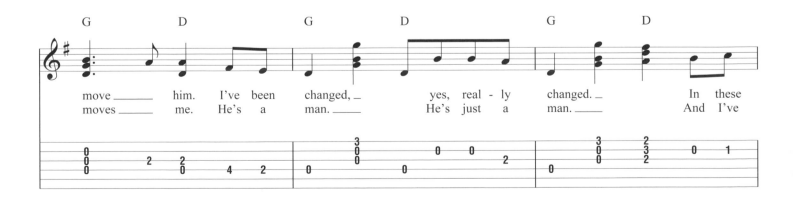

move _____ him. I've been changed, ___ yes, real - ly changed. ___ In these
moves _____ me. He's a man. _____ He's just a man. _____ And I've

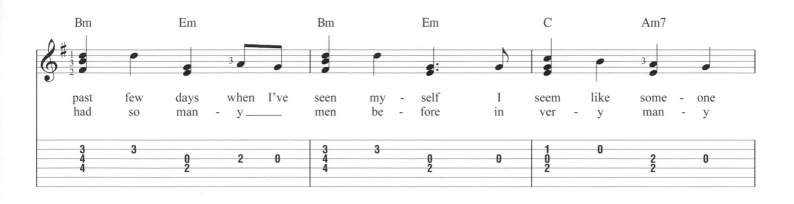

past few days when I've seen my - self I seem like some - one
had so man - y men be - fore in ver - y man - y

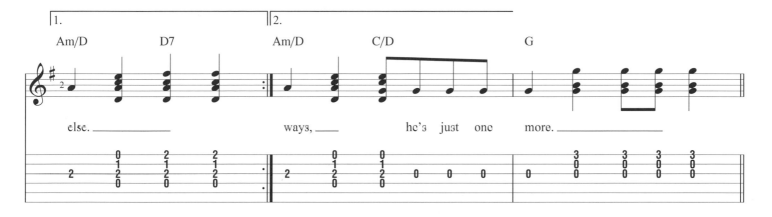

1.
else. _____

2.
ways, _____ he's just one more. _____

Bridge

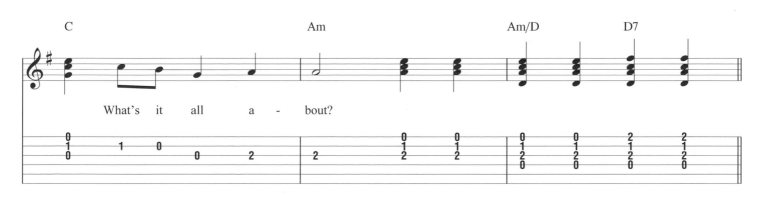

Should I bring him down? Should I scream and shout? Should I speak of

love, let my feel - ings out? I nev - er thought I'd come to this.

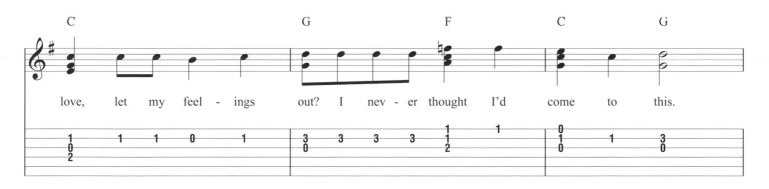

What's it all a - bout?

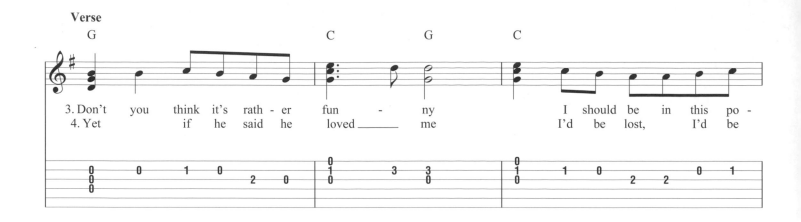

3. Don't you think it's rath - er fun - ny I should be in this po -
4. Yet if he said he loved _____ me I'd be lost, I'd be

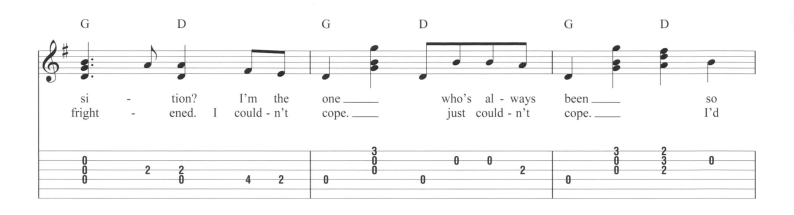

si - tion? I'm the one _____ who's al - ways been _____ so
fright - ened. I could - n't cope. _____ just could - n't cope. _____ I'd

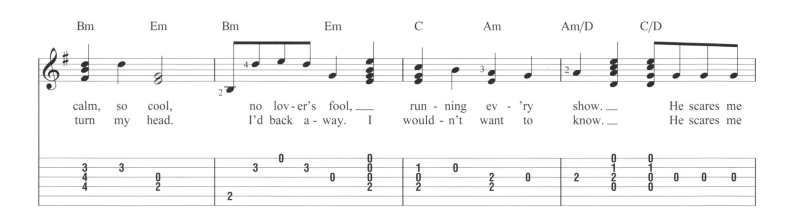

calm, so cool, no lov - er's fool, ___ run - ning ev - 'ry show. __ He scares me
turn my head. I'd back a - way. I would - n't want to know. __ He scares me

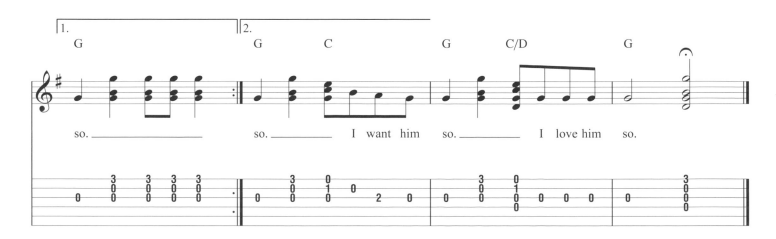

1.   2.
so. _____   so. _____ I want him so. _____ I love him so.

I Dreamed a Dream

from LES MISÉRABLES

Music by Claude-Michel Schönberg

Lyrics by Alain Boublil, Jean-Marc Natel and Herbert Kretzmer

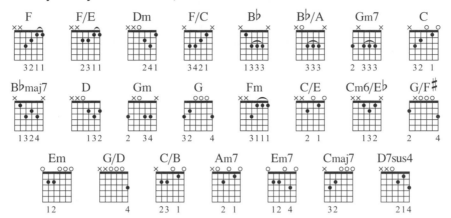

Strum Pattern: 3, 4
Pick Pattern: 3, 3

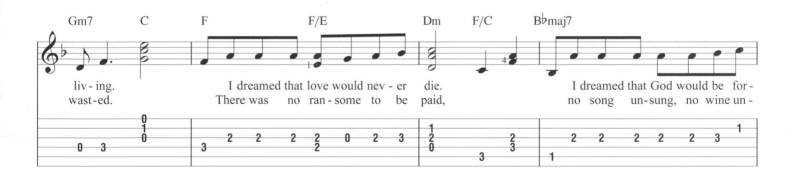

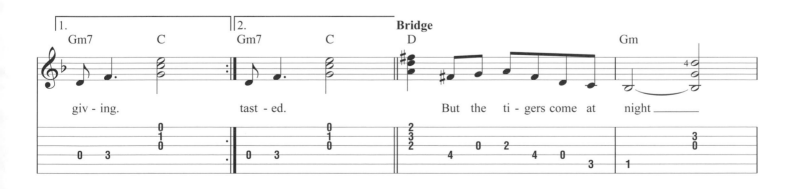

Music and French Lyrics Copyright © 1980 by Editions Musicales Alain Boublil
English Lyrics Copyright © 1986 by Alain Boublil Music Ltd. (ASCAP)
Mechanical and Publication Rights for the U.S.A. Administered by Alain Boublil Music Ltd. (ASCAP) c/o Spielman Koenigsberg & Parker, LLP,
Richard Koenigsberg, 1675 Broadway, 20th Floor, New York, NY 10019, Tel 212-453-2500, Fax 212-453-2550, ABML@skpny.com

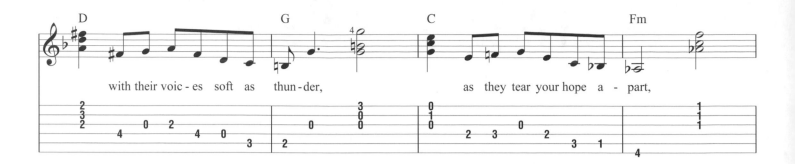

with their voic - es soft as thun - der, as they tear your hope a - part,

as they turn your dream to shame. _____

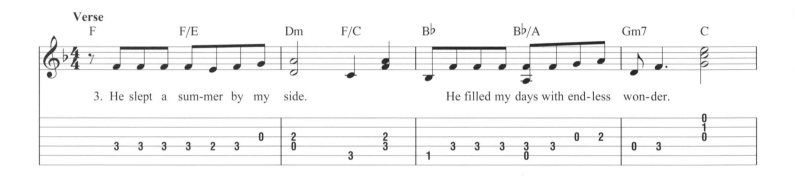

Verse

3. He slept a sum - mer by my side. He filled my days with end - less won - der.

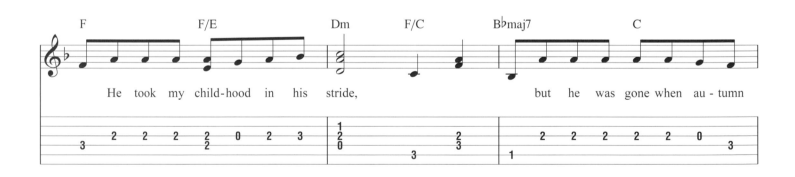

He took my child-hood in his stride, but he was gone when au - tumn

came. __ **Verse** 4. And still I dreamed he'd come to me,

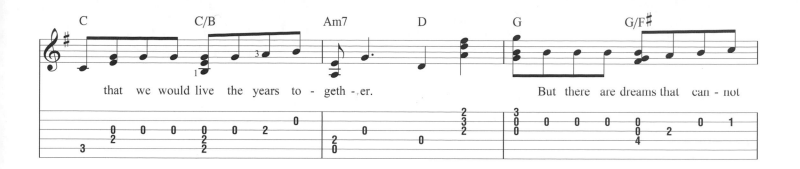

that we would live the years to - geth - er.   But there are dreams that can - not

be,   and there are storms we can - not weath - er.

I had a dream my life would be ____

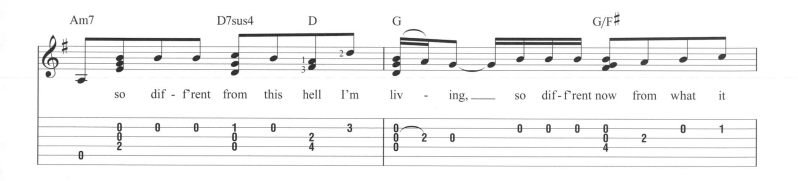

so dif - f'rent from this hell I'm liv - ing, ____ so dif - f'rent now from what it

seemed.   Now life has killed the dream I dreamed. ____

If I Were a Bell

from GUYS AND DOLLS

By Frank Loesser

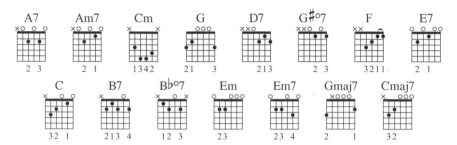

Strum Pattern: 3
Pick Pattern: 3

Verse

Moderately

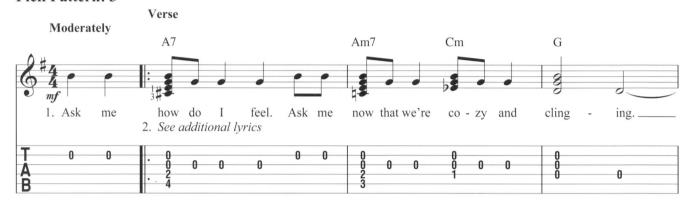

1. Ask me how do I feel. Ask me now that we're co-zy and cling-ing. _____
2. *See additional lyrics*

_____ Well, sir, all I can say is if I were a bell, I'd be ring-ing. _____

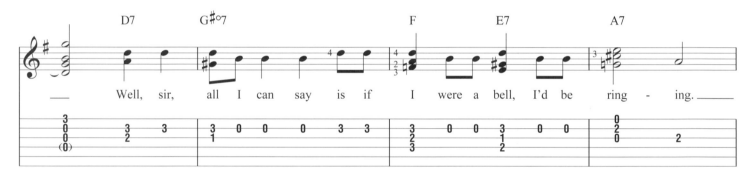

_____ From the mo-ment we kissed to-night, that's the way I've just got to be-

have. Boy, if I were a lamp, I'd light, or if I were a ban-ner, I'd

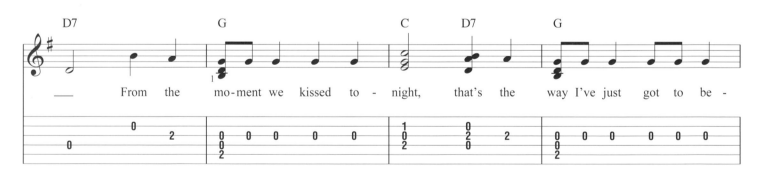

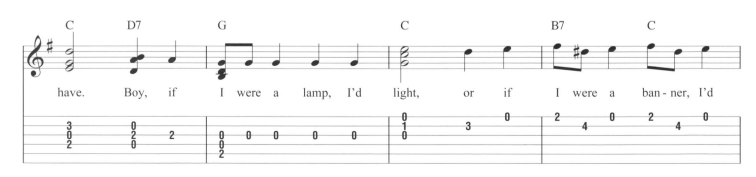

Additional Lyrics

2. Ask me how do I feel from this chemistry lesson I'm learning.
Will, sir, all I can say is if I were a bridge, I'd be burning.
Yes, I knew my morale would crack from the wonderful way that you looked.
Boy, if I were a duck, I'd quack, or if I were a goose, I'd be cooked.
Ask me how do I feel, ask me now that we're fondly caressing.
Pal, if I were a salad, I know I'd be splashing my dressing.
Or if I were a season, I'd surely be spring.
Or if I were a bell, I'd go ding, dong, ding, dong, ding.

Mamma Mia

featured in MAMMA MIA!

Words and Music by Benny Andersson, Björn Ulvaeus and Stig Anderson

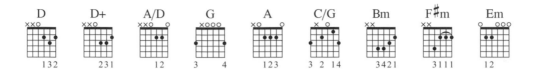

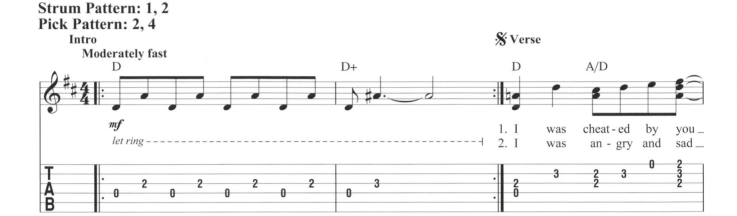

Strum Pattern: 1, 2
Pick Pattern: 2, 4

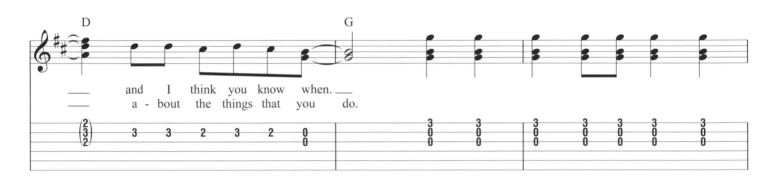

and I think you know when. ___
a - bout the things that you do.

So   I   made up   my mind ___   it   must come to   an   end. ___
I   can't count all   the times ___ that   I've cried o - ver   you. ___

Look   at   me   now, ___   will   I   ev - er   learn?
And when you   go, ___   when you slam the door

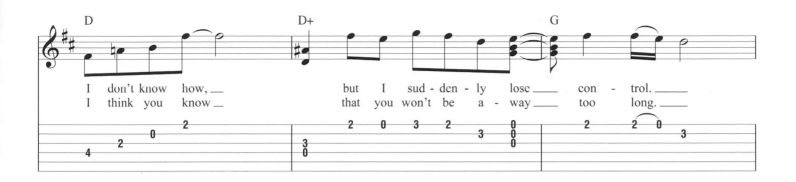

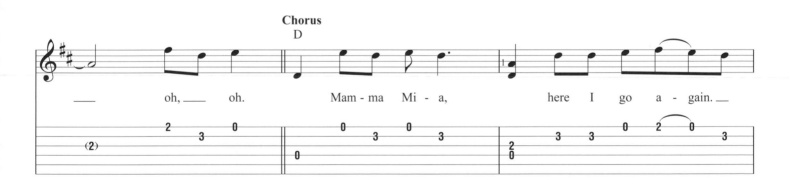

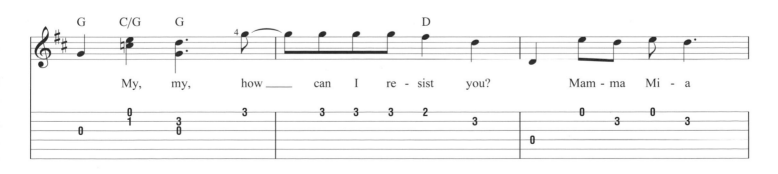

Memory

from CATS
Music by Andrew Lloyd Webber
Text by Trevor Nunn after T.S. Eliot

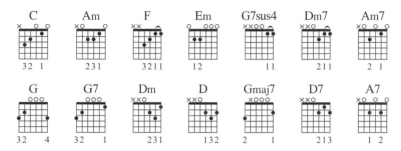

Strum Pattern: 8
Pick Pattern: 8

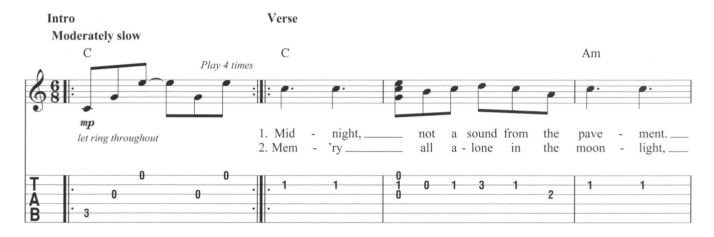

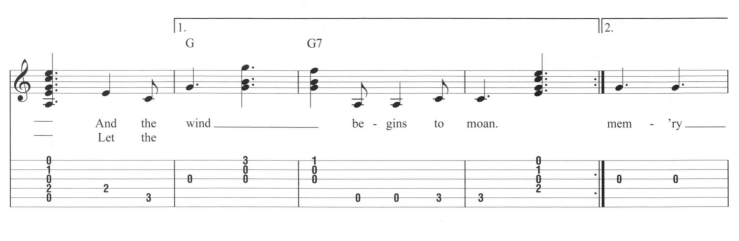

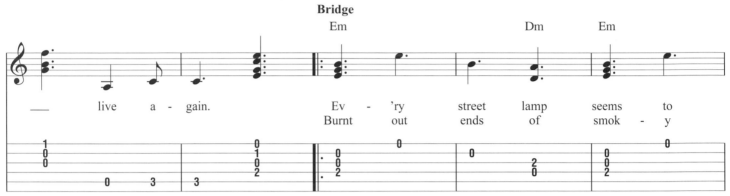

Bridge

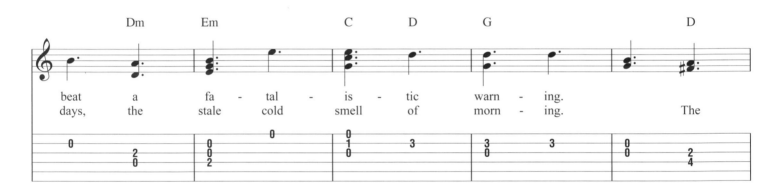

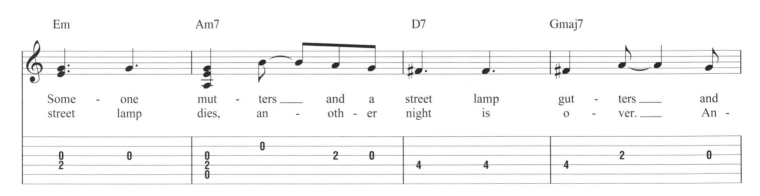

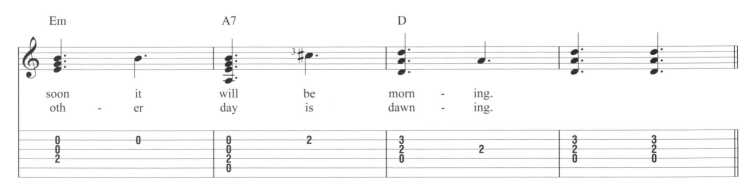

Verse

3. Day - light, _____ I must wait for the sun - rise. _____ I must think of a
4. Touch me. _____ It's so eas - y to leave me _____ all a - lone with this

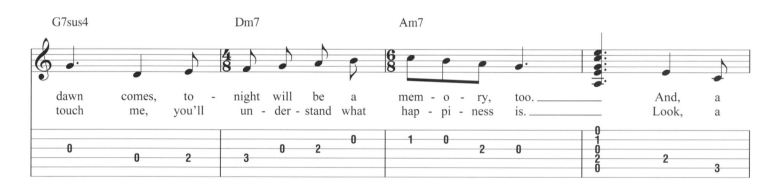

new life _____ and I must - n't give in. _____ When the
mem - 'ry _____ of my days in the sun. _____ If you

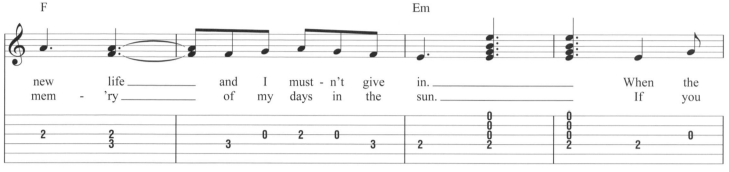

dawn comes, to - night will be a mem - o - ry, too. _____ And, a
touch me, you'll un - der - stand what hap - pi - ness is. _____ Look, a

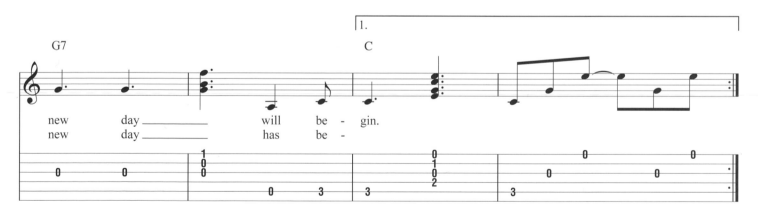

|1.

new day _____ will be - gin.
new day _____ has be -

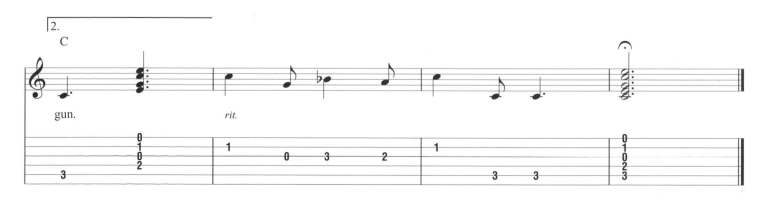

|2.

gun.   *rit.*

Popular

from the Broadway Musical WICKED
Music and Lyrics by Stephen Schwartz

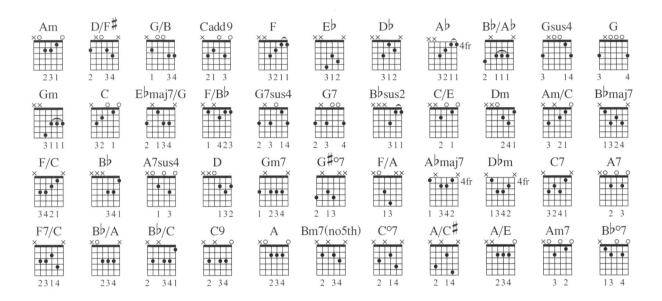

Strum Pattern: 4, 3
Pick Pattern: 1

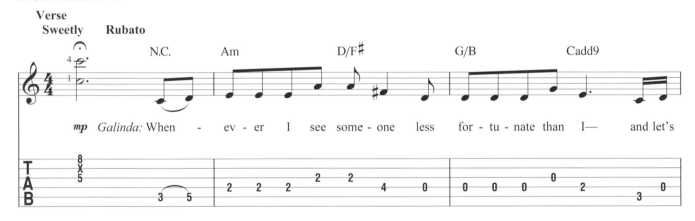

Galinda: When - ev - er I see some - one less for - tu - nate than I— and let's

face it, who is - n't less for - tu - nate than I? My ten - der heart tends to start to

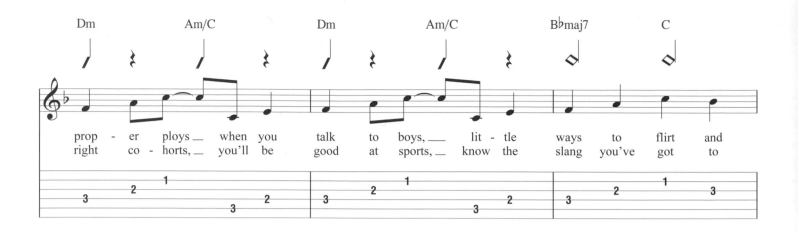

prop - er ploys __ when you talk to boys, __ lit - tle ways to flirt and
right co - horts, __ you'll be good at sports, __ know the slang you've got to

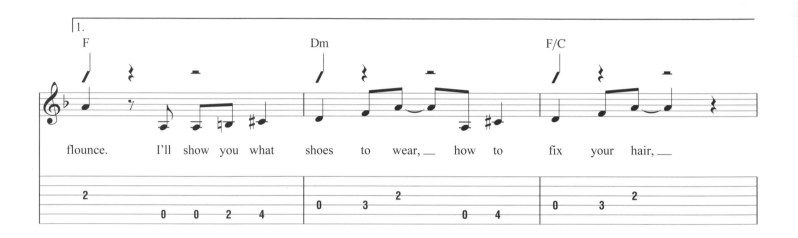

1.

flounce. I'll show you what shoes to wear, __ how to fix your hair, __

2.

ev - 'ry thing that real - ly counts __ to be know. So let's

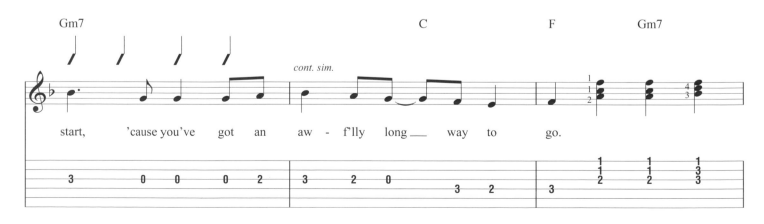

start, 'cause you've got an aw - f'lly long __ way to go.

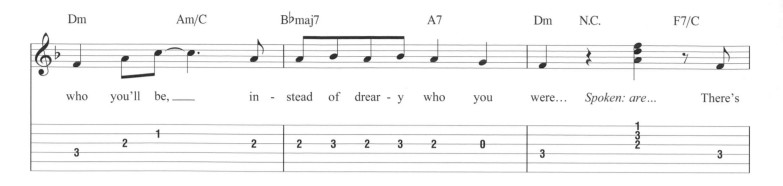

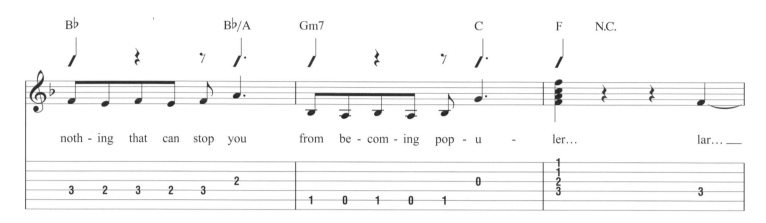

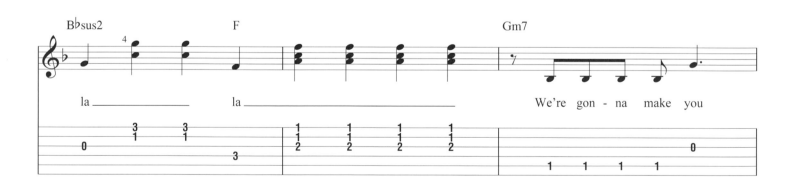

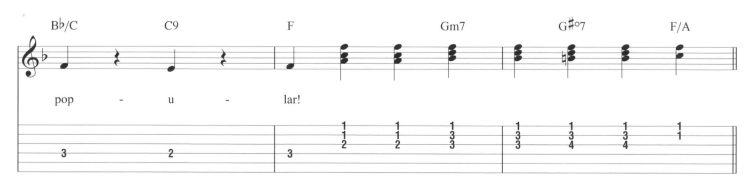

Bridge

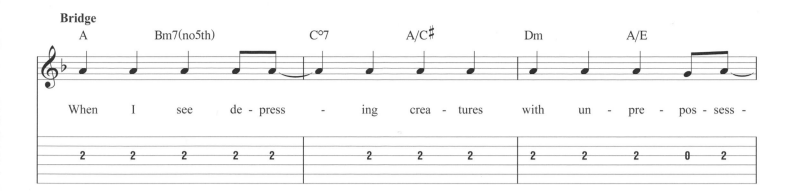

When I see de - press - ing crea - tures with un - pre - pos - sess -

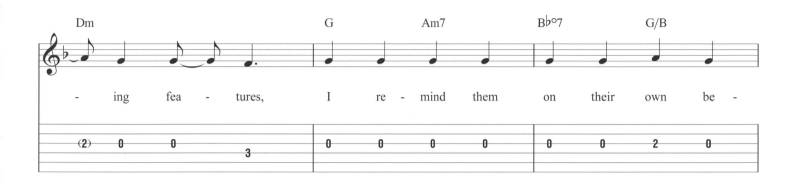

- ing fea - tures, I re - mind them on their own be -

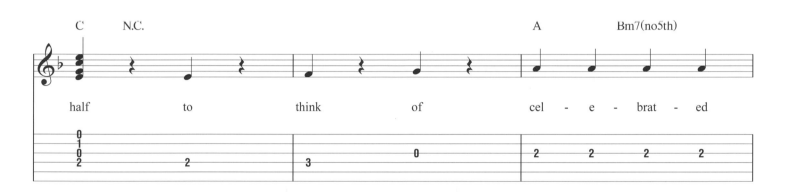

half to think of cel - e - brat - ed

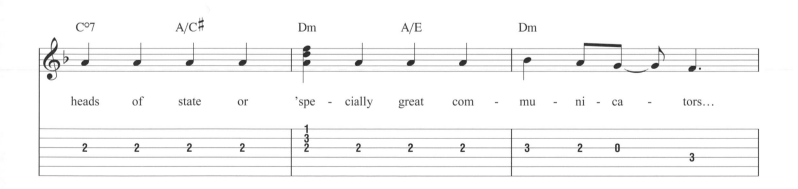

heads of state or 'spe - cially great com - mu - ni - ca - tors...

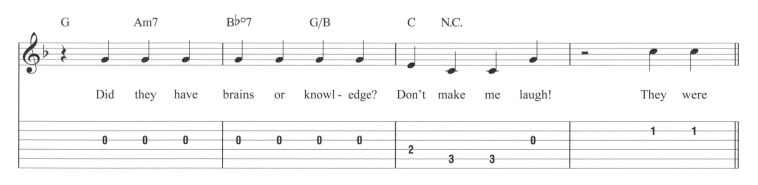

Did they have brains or knowl - edge? Don't make me laugh! They were

Chorus

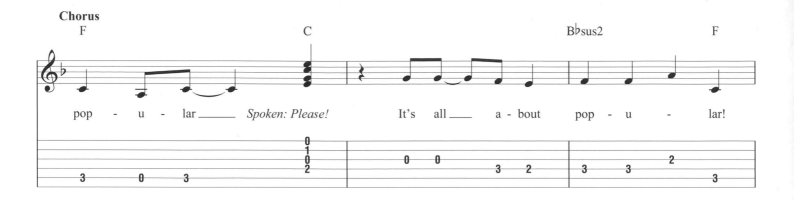

pop - u - lar _____ *Spoken: Please!* It's all _____ a - bout pop - u - lar!

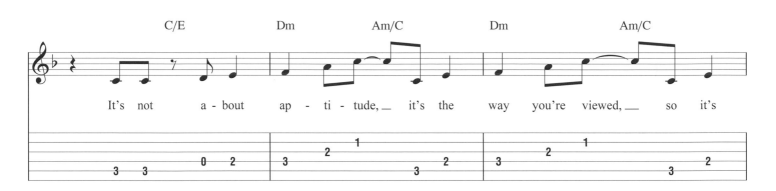

It's not a - bout ap - ti - tude, _____ it's the way you're viewed, _____ so it's

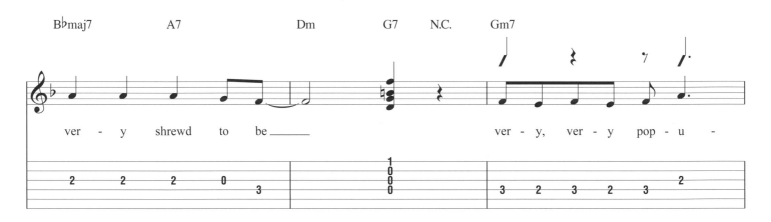

ver - y shrewd to be _____ ver - y, ver - y pop - u -

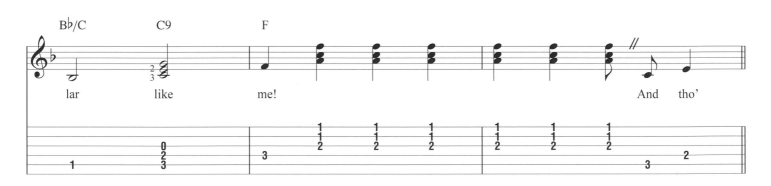

lar like me! And tho'

Outro
Freely

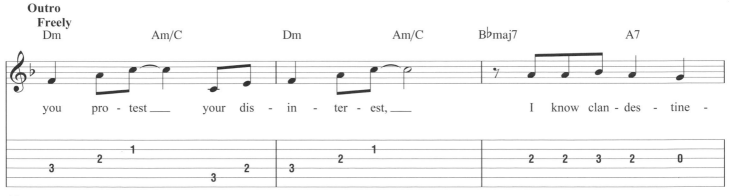

you pro - test _____ your dis - in - ter - est, _____ I know clan - des - tine -

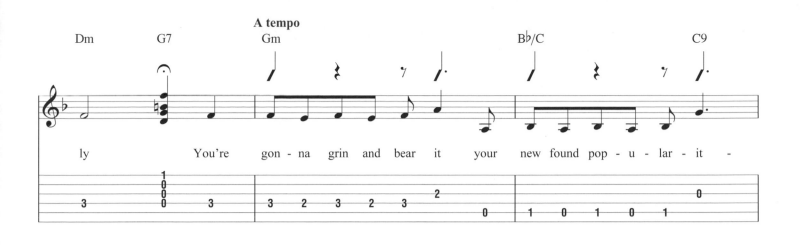

ly   You're gon - na grin and bear it   your new found pop - u - lar - it -

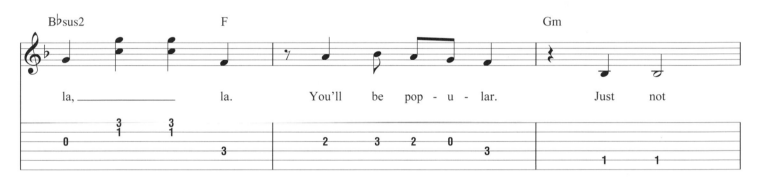

y.   La, _____ la, _____

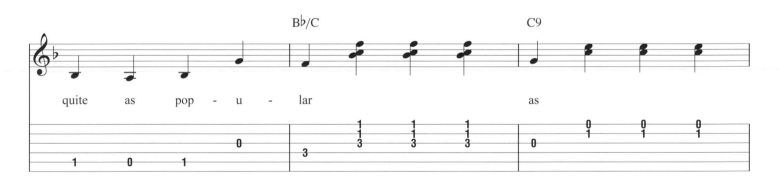

la, _____ la.   You'll be pop - u - lar.   Just not

quite as pop - u - lar   as

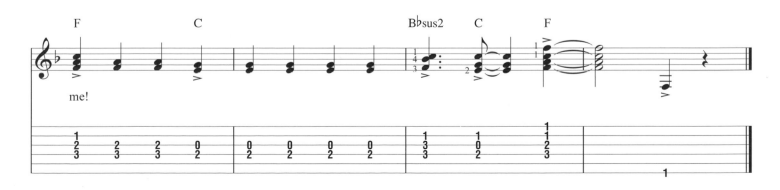

me!

Seasons of Love

from RENT

Words and Music by Jonathan Larson

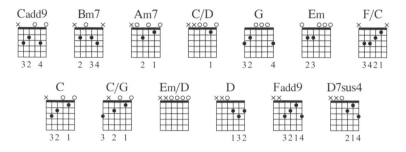

*Tune down 1 step:
(low to high) D-G-C-F-A-D

Strum Pattern: 6
Pick Pattern: 4

Intro
Moderately

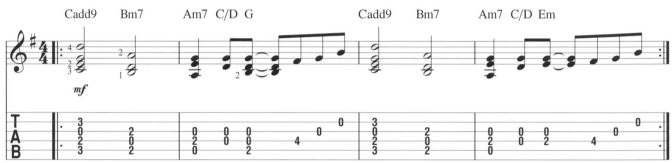

*Optional: To match recording, tune down 1 step.

Verse

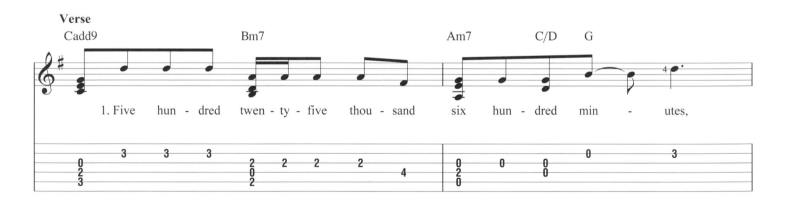

1. Five hun-dred twen-ty-five thou-sand six hun-dred min-utes,

five hun-dred twen-ty-five thou-sand mo-ments so dear. _____

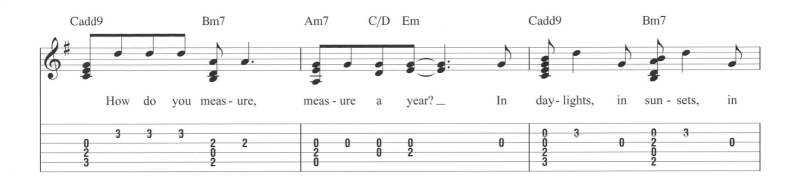

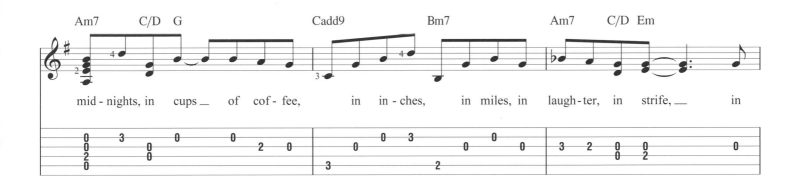

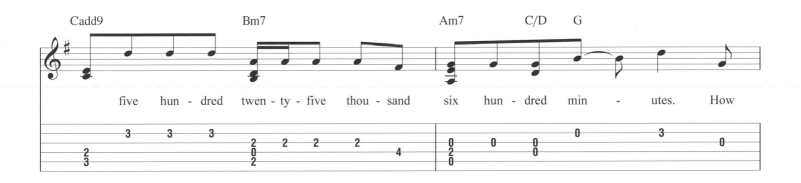

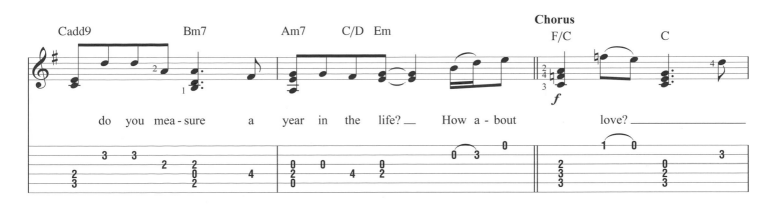

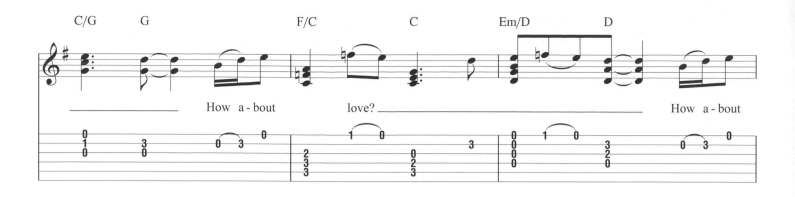

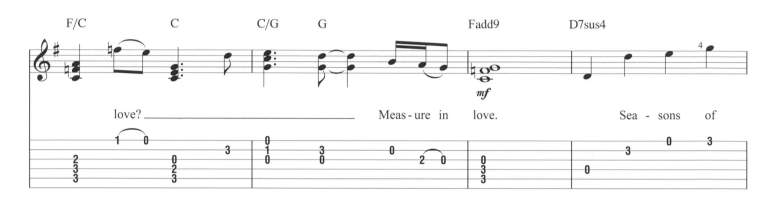

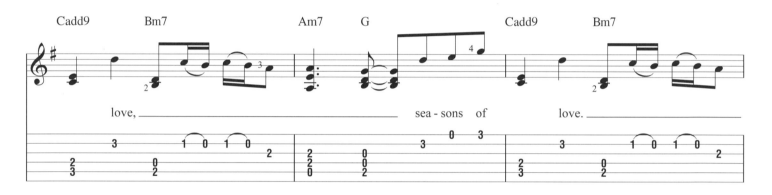

Verse

*2nd Verse sung one octave higher than written, next 8 meas.

Five hun - dred twen - ty - five thou - sand six hun - dred min - utes. How __

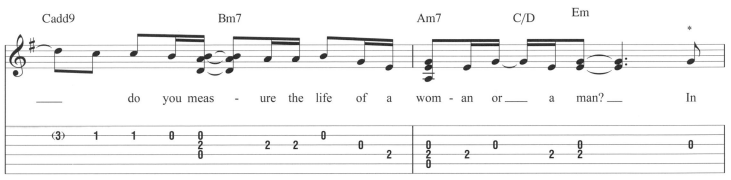

__ do you meas - ure the life of a wom - an or __ a man? __ In

*Sung as written.

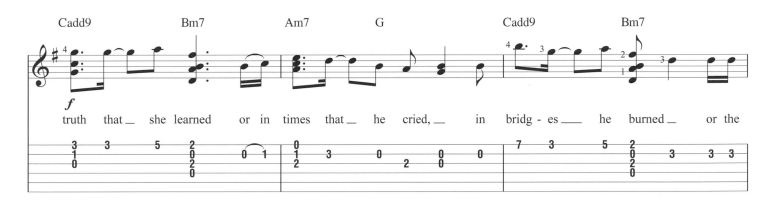

truth that __ she learned or in times that __ he cried, __ in bridg - es __ he burned __ or the

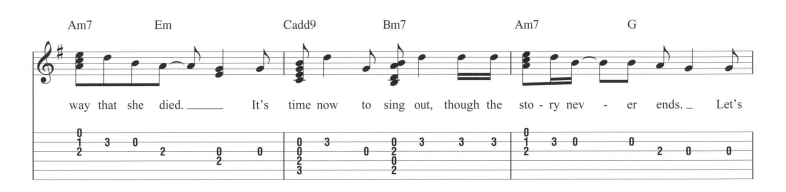

way that she died. __ It's time now to sing out, though the sto - ry nev - er ends. __ Let's

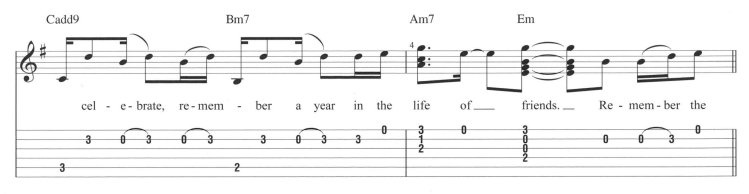

cel - e - brate, re - mem - ber a year in the life of __ friends. __ Re - mem - ber the

Chorus

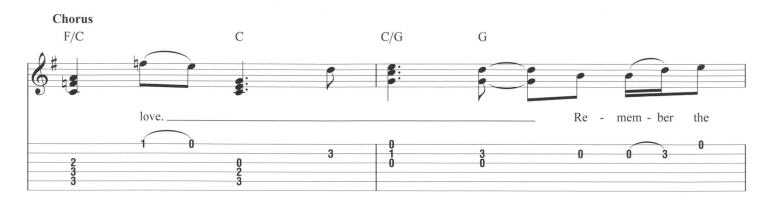

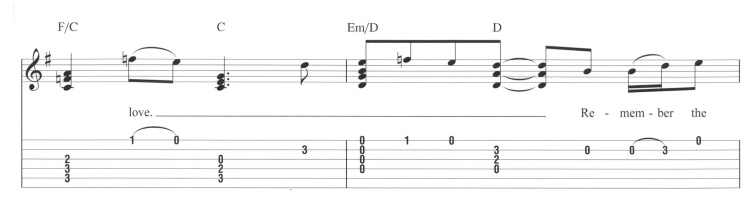

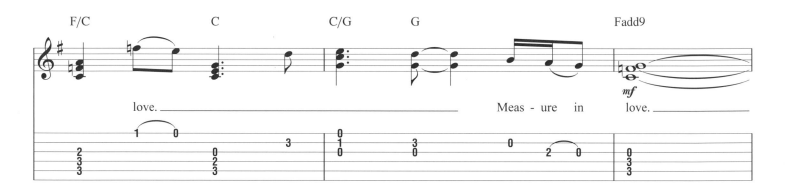

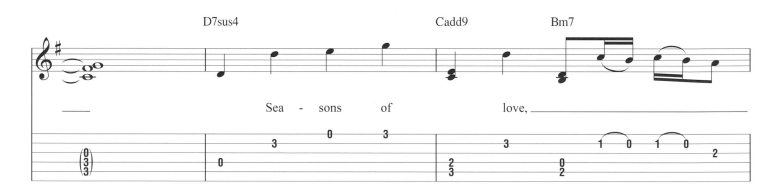

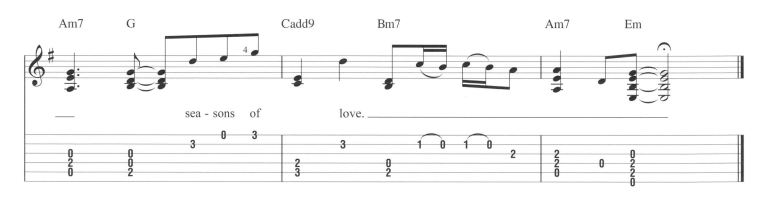

She Used to Be Mine

from WAITRESS THE MUSICAL

Words and Music by Sara Bareilles

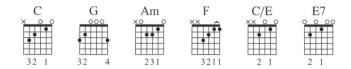

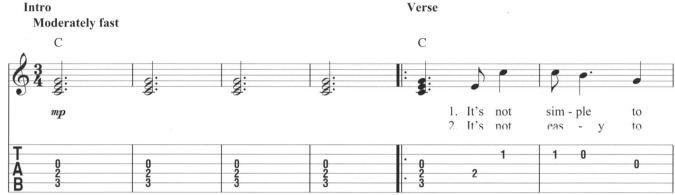

*Capo V

Strum Pattern: 8
Pick Pattern: 8

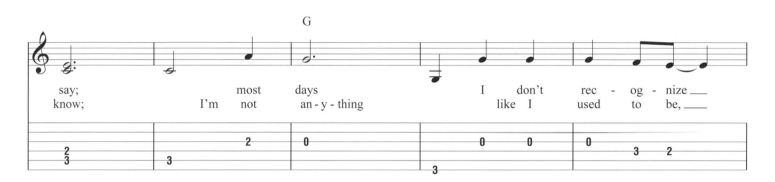

*Optional: To match recording, place capo at 5th fret.

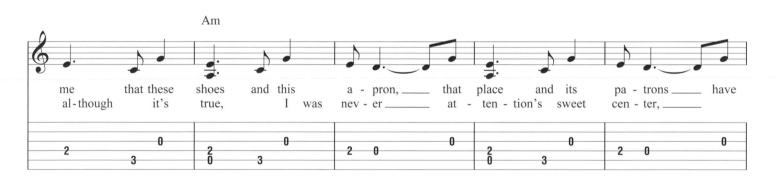

Chorus

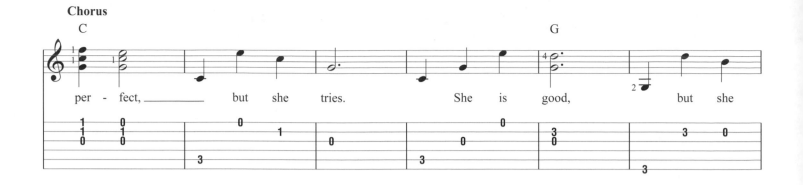

per - fect, _____ but she tries. She is good, _____ but she

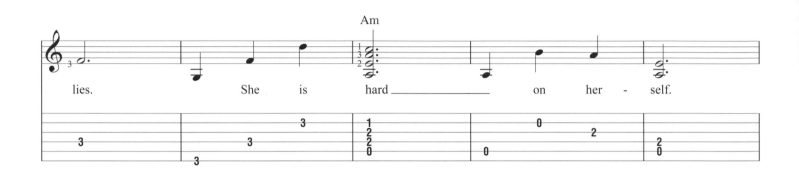

lies. She is hard _____ on her - self.

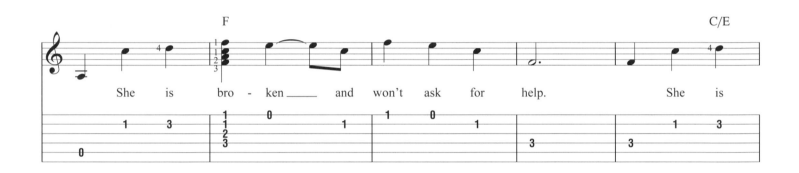

She is bro - ken _____ and won't ask for help. She is

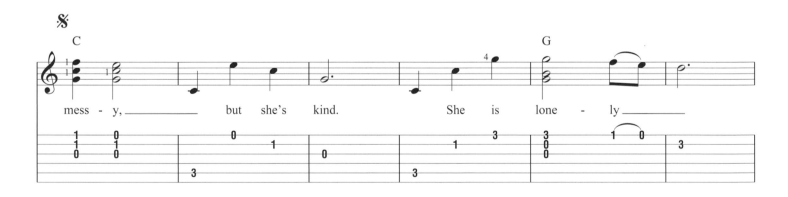

mess - y, _____ but she's kind. She is lone - ly _____

most of the time. _____ She is all of this, _ mixed up and baked in a

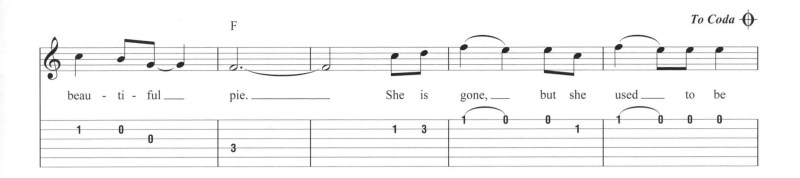

beau - ti - ful ___ pie. _____ She is gone, ___ but she used ___ to be

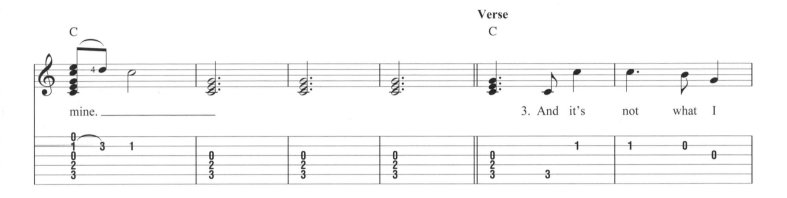

mine. _____ 3. And it's not what I

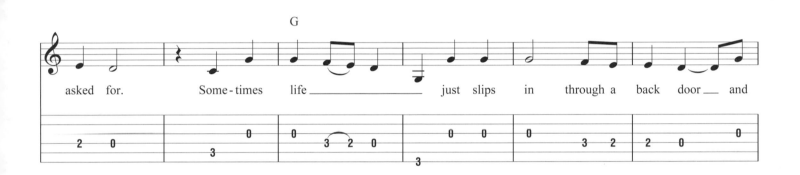

asked for. Some - times life _____ just slips in through a back door ___ and

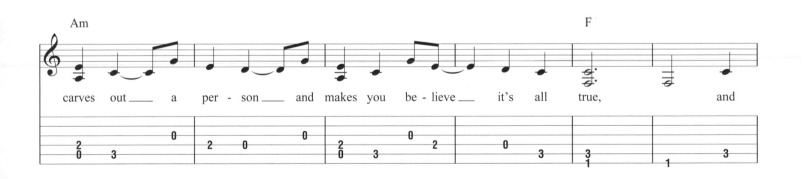

carves out ___ a per - son ___ and makes you be - lieve ___ it's all true, and

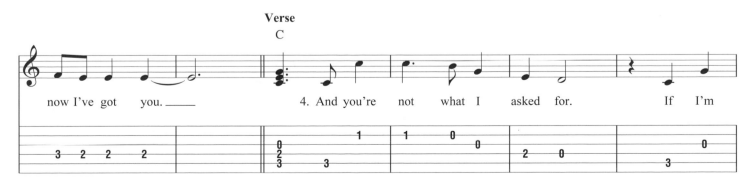

now I've got you. ___ 4. And you're not what I asked for. If I'm

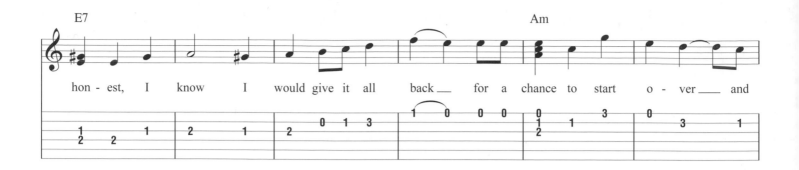

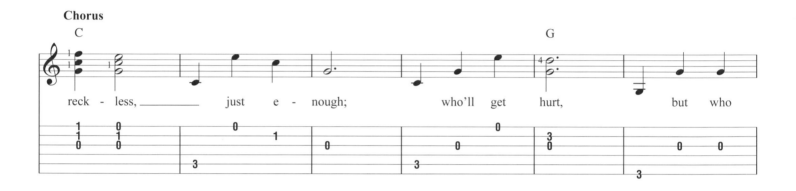

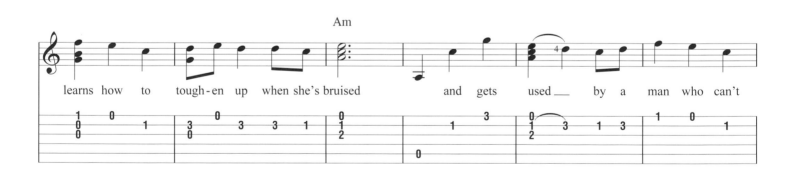

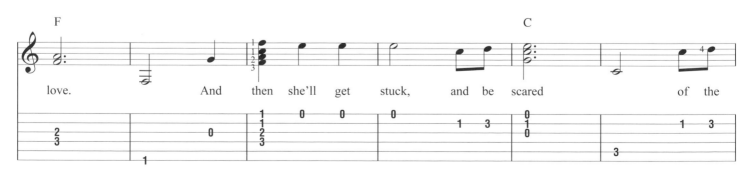

life that's in - side her, grow - ing strong - er each _ day, till it fi - n'lly re - minds _ her to

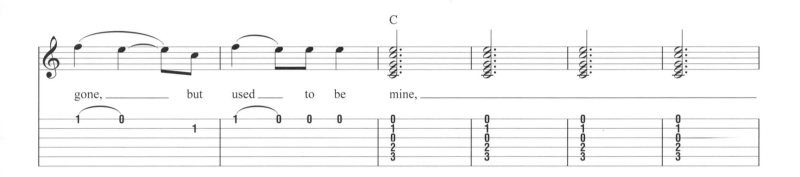

fight just a lit - tle to bring back the fire in her eyes _____ that's been

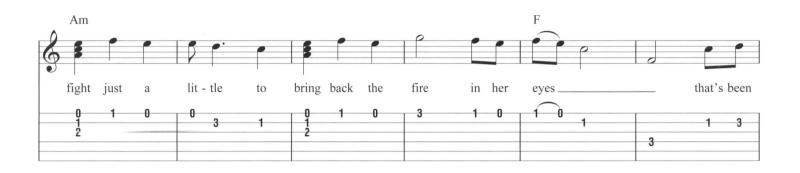

gone, _____ but used ___ to be mine, _____

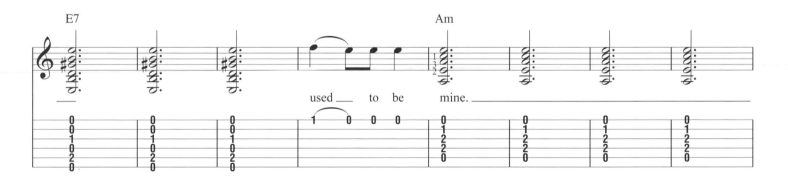

used ___ to be mine. _____

D.S. al Coda   ⊕ **Coda**

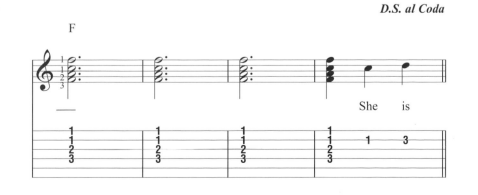

She is

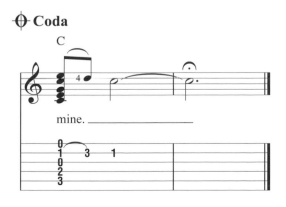

mine. _____

Summertime

from PORGY AND BESS®

Music and Lyrics by George Gershwin, DuBose and Dorothy Heyward and Ira Gershwin

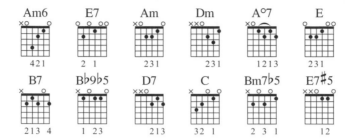

Strum Pattern: 3
Pick Pattern: 3

Verse
Slow

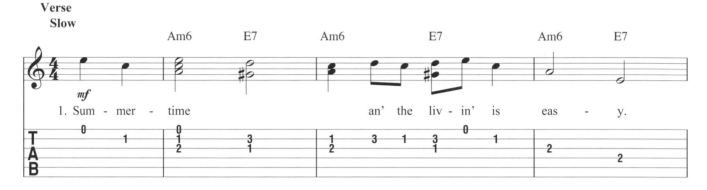

1. Sum - mer - time an' the liv - in' is eas - y.

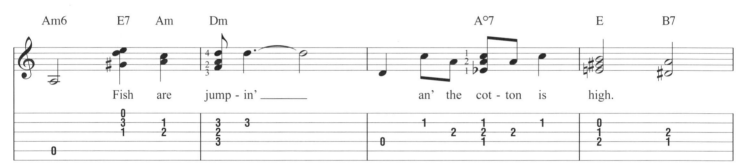

Fish are jump - in' _____ an' the cot - ton is high.

Oh, yo' dad - dy's rich, an' yo' ma is good

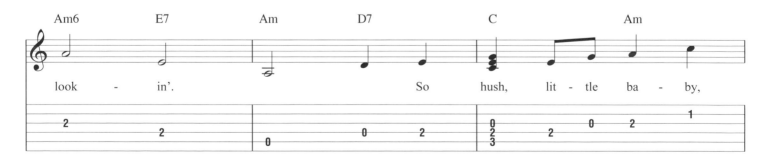

look - in'. So hush, lit - tle ba - by,

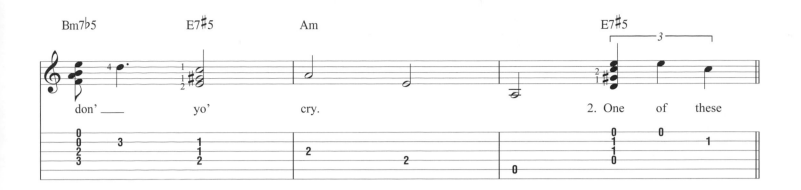

don' ___ yo' cry. 2. One of these

Verse

morn - in's you go'n' to rise ___ up sing - in'. Then you'll

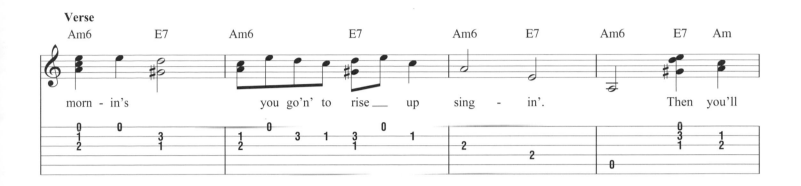

spread your wings ___ an' you'll take ___ the sky. But till that

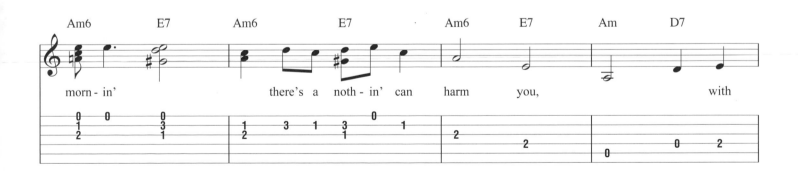

morn - in' there's a noth - in' can harm you, with

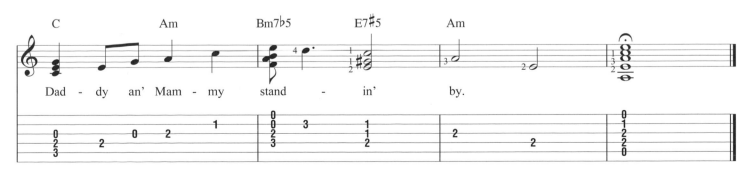

Dad - dy an' Mam - my stand - in' by.

Sunrise, Sunset

from the Musical FIDDLER ON THE ROOF
Words by Sheldon Harnick
Music by Jerry Bock

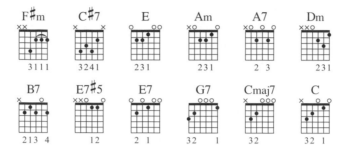

Strum Pattern: 8
Pick Pattern: 8

Intro
Moderately slow

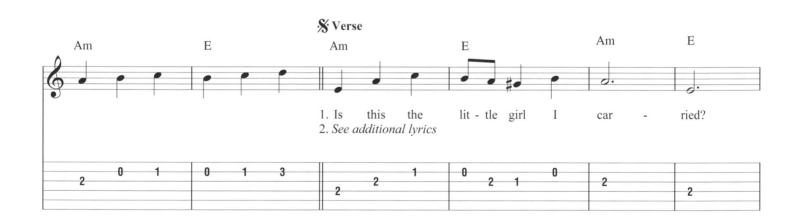

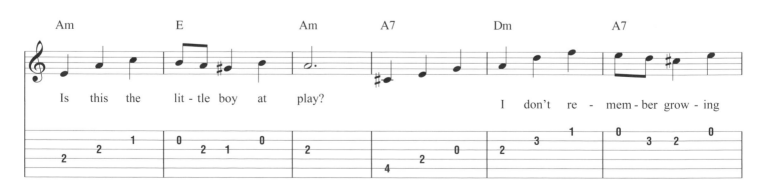

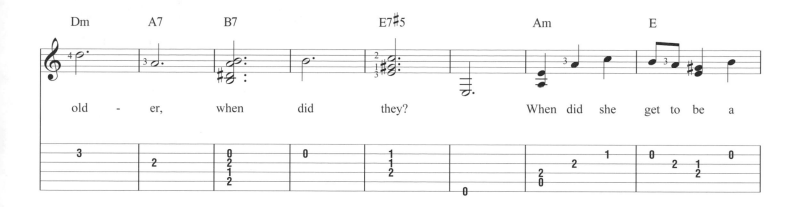

old - er,   when   did   they?   When did she   get to be   a

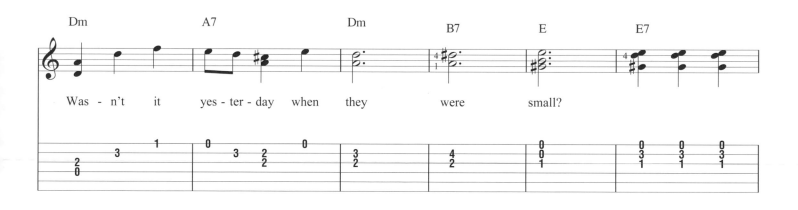

beau - ty?   When   did   he   grow   to   be   so   tall?

Was - n't   it   yes - ter - day   when   they   were   small?

Chorus

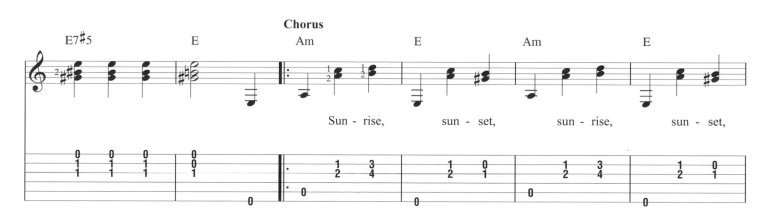

Sun - rise,   sun - set,   sun - rise,   sun - set,

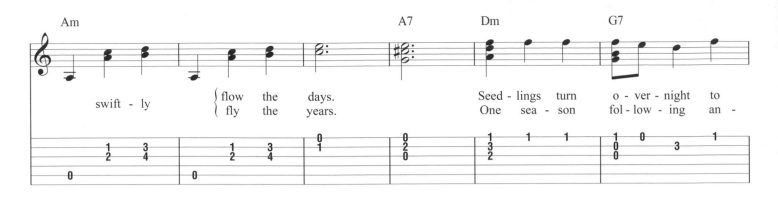

swift - ly {flow the days. / fly the years.} Seed - lings turn o - ver - night to / One sea - son fol - low - ing an -

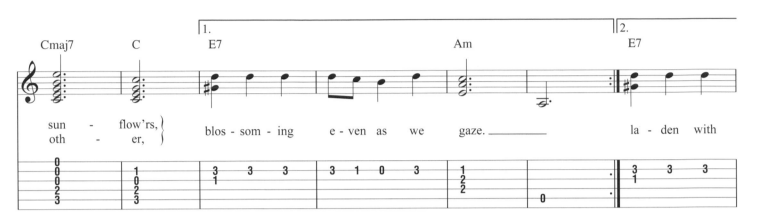

{sun - flow'rs, / oth - er,} blos - som - ing e - ven as we gaze._____ la - den with

To Coda ⊕

Interlude

D.S. al Coda
(take 2nd ending)

⊕ **Coda**

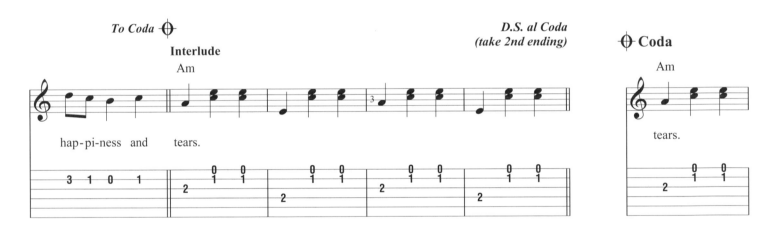

hap-pi-ness and tears.

tears.

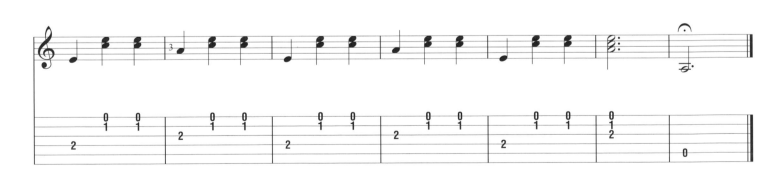

Additional Lyrics

2. What words of wisdom can I give them?
How can I help to ease their way?
Now they must learn from one another,
Day by day.
They look so natural together,
Just like two newlyweds should be.
Is there a canopy in
Store for me?

The Surrey with the Fringe on Top

from OKLAHOMA!

Lyrics by Oscar Hammerstein II
Music by Richard Rodgers

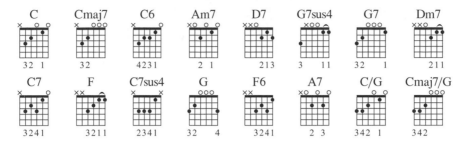

Strum Pattern: 3
Pick Pattern: 3

Verse
Fast

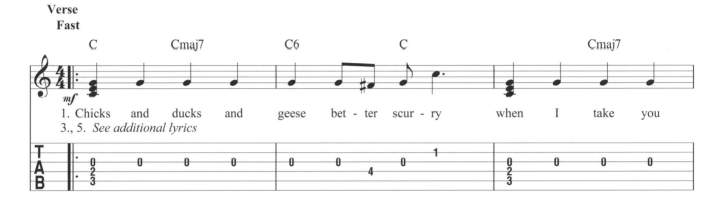

1. Chicks and ducks and geese bet-ter scur-ry when I take you
3., 5. *See additional lyrics*

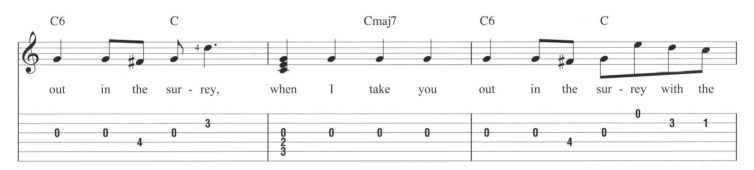

out in the sur-rey, when I take you out in the sur-rey with the

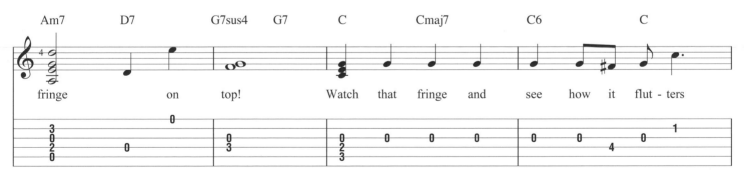

fringe on top! Watch that fringe and see how it flut-ters

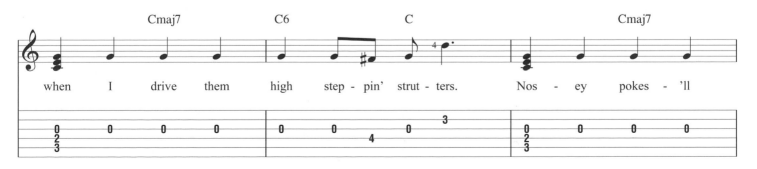

when I drive them high step-pin' strut-ters. Nos-ey pokes-'ll

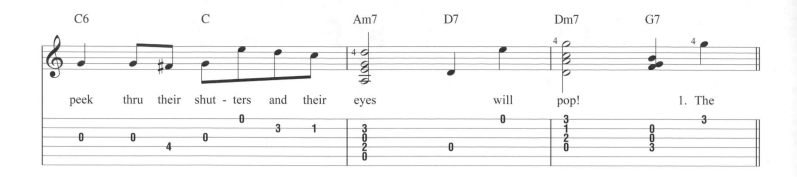

peek thru their shut - ters and their eyes will pop! 1. The

Bridge

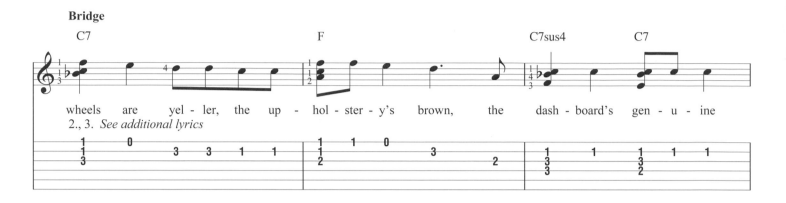

wheels are yel - ler, the up - hol - ster - y's brown, the dash - board's gen - u - ine

2., 3. See additional lyrics

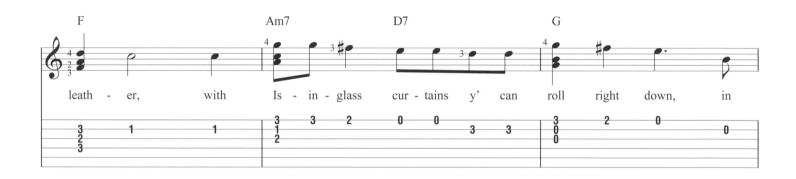

leath - er, with Is - in - glass cur - tains y' can roll right down, in

Verse

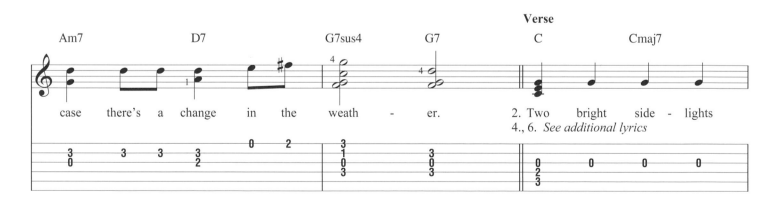

case there's a change in the weath - er. 2. Two bright side - lights

4., 6. See additional lyrics

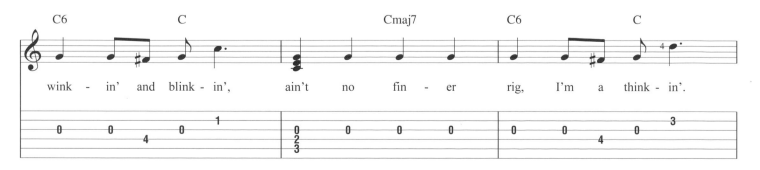

wink - in' and blink - in', ain't no fin - er rig, I'm a think - in'.

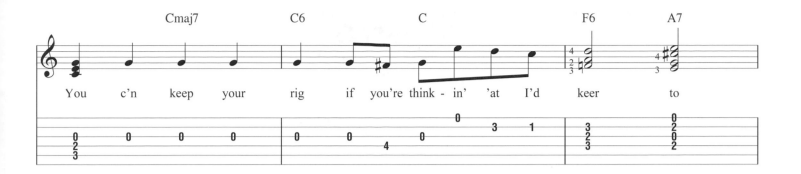

You c'n keep your rig if you're think-in' 'at I'd keer to

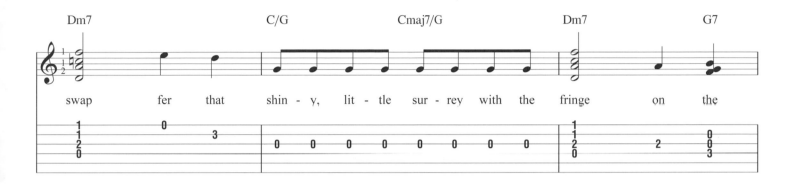

swap fer that shin-y, lit-tle sur-rey with the fringe on the

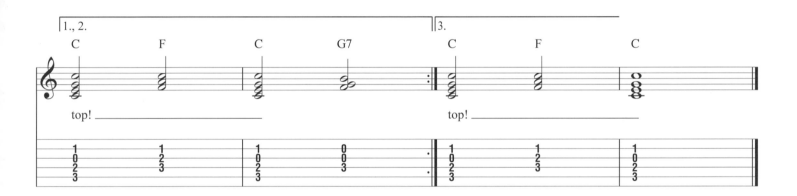

top! _____ top! _____

Additional Lyrics

3. All the world'll fly in a flurry when I take you out in the surrey,
   When I take you out in the surrey with the fringe on top!
   When we hit that road, hell fer leather, cats and dogs'll dance in the heather,
   Birds and frogs'll sing all together and the toads will hop!

Bridge 2 The winds will whistle as we rattle along, the cows'll moo in the clover,
   The river will ripple out a whispered song, and whisper it over and over.

4. Don't you wisht y'd go on forever? Don't you wisht y'd go on forever?
   Don't you wisht y'd go on forever and ud never stop
   In that shiny, little surrey with the fringe on the top!

5. I can see the stars gettin' blurry when we drive back home in the surrey,
   Drivin' slowly home in the surrey with the fringe on top!
   I can feel the day gettin' older, feel a sleepy head on my shoulder,
   Noddin', droopin' close to my shoulder till it falls kerplop!

Bridge 3 The sun is swimmin' on the rim of the hill, the moon is takin' a header,
   And jist as I'm thinkin' all the earth is still, a lark'll wake up in the medder.

6. Hush, you bird, my baby's a sleepin'! Maybe got a dream worth a keepin'.
   Whoa! You team, and jist keep a creepin' at a slow clip clop.
   Don't you hurry with the surrey with the fringe on the top!

Tomorrow

from the Musical Production ANNIE
Lyric by Martin Charnin
Music by Charles Strouse

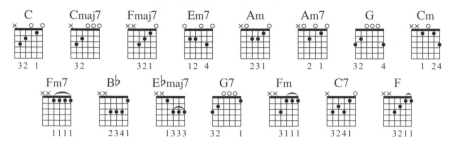

Strum Pattern: 4
Pick Pattern: 4

Verse
Moderately slow

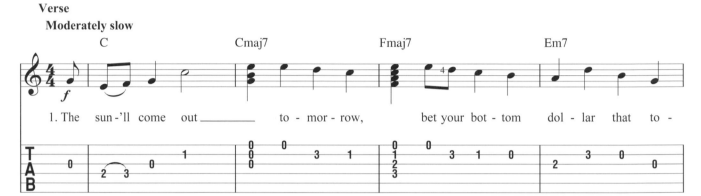

1. The sun-'ll come out _____ to-mor-row, bet your bot-tom dol-lar that to-

mor-row _____ there'll be sun! _____ 2. Jus'

Verse

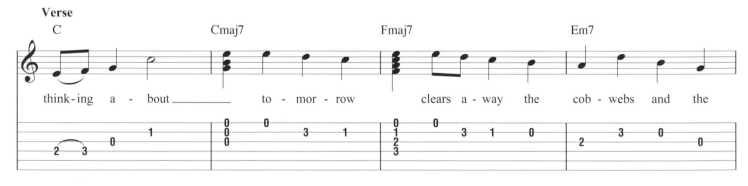

think-ing a-bout _____ to-mor-row clears a-way the cob-webs and the

sor-row _____ till there's none. _____ When I'm stuck _____ with a

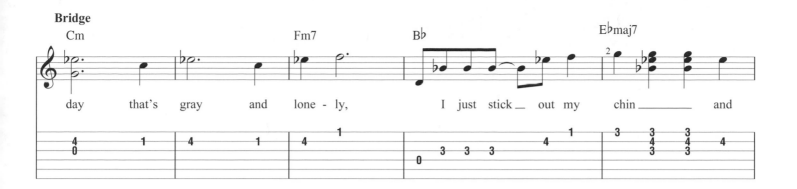

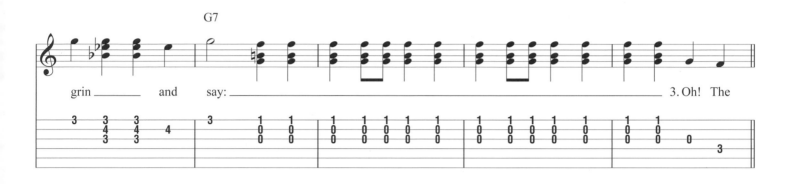

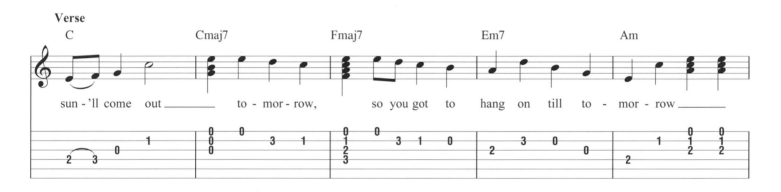

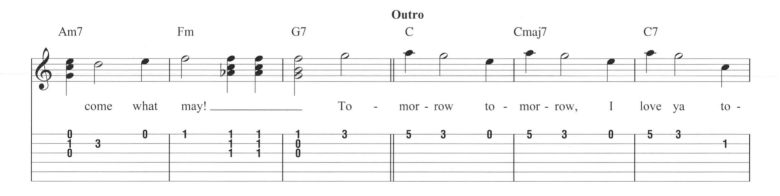

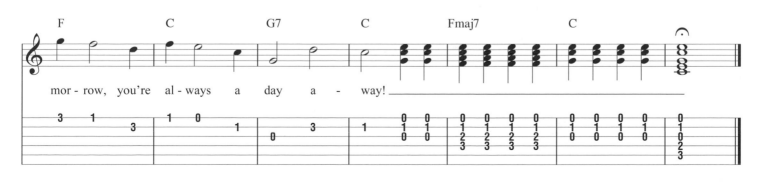

Waving Through a Window

from DEAR EVAN HANSEN

Music and Lyrics by Benj Pasek and Justin Paul

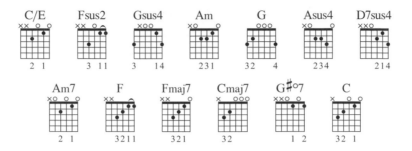

Strum Pattern: 3, 6
Pick Pattern: 3, 5

Intro
Moderately fast

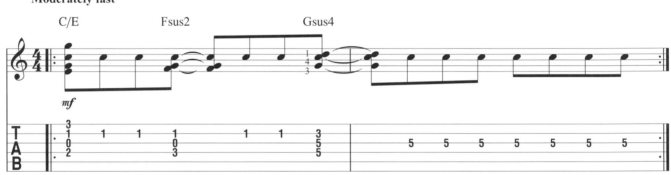

Verse

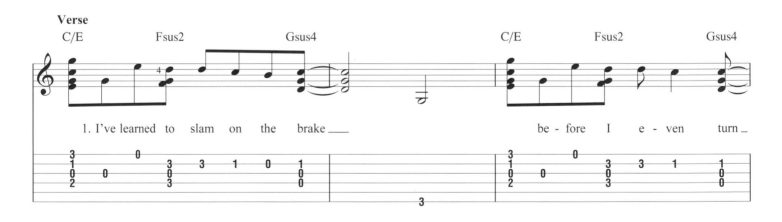

1. I've learned to slam on the brake ___ before I e - ven turn ___

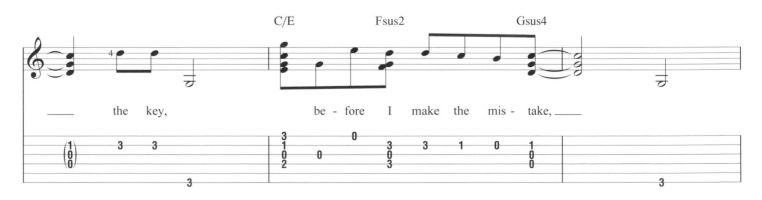

___ the key, before I make the mis - take, ___

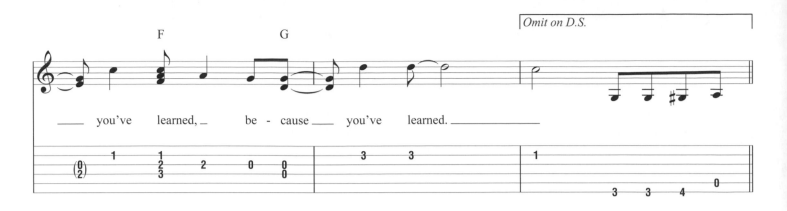

℅℅ Chorus

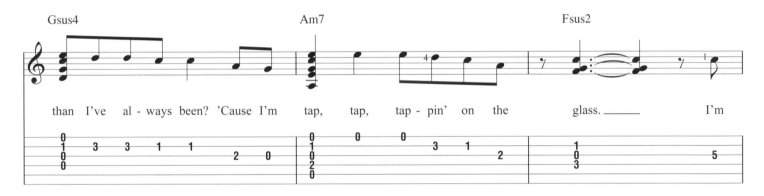

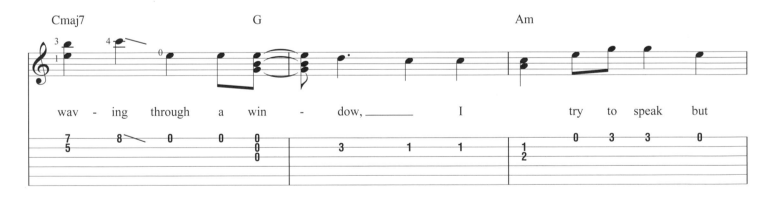

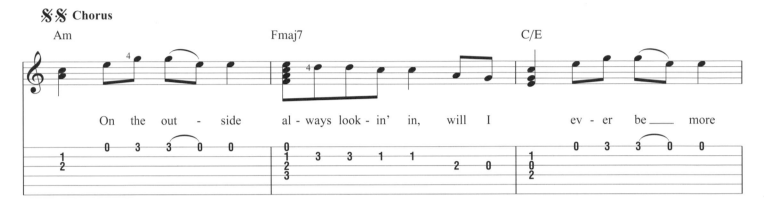

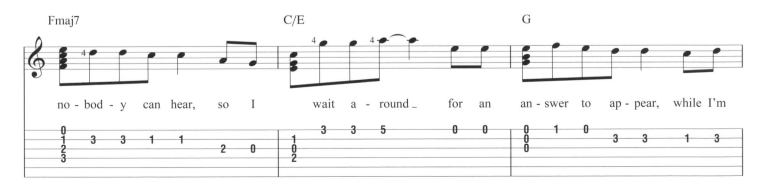

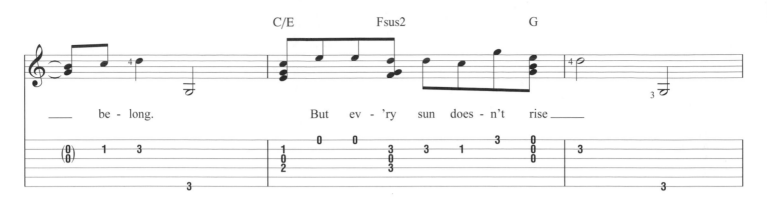

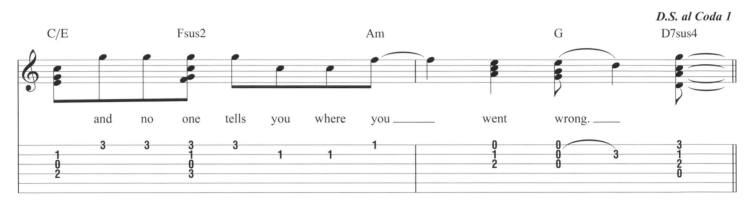

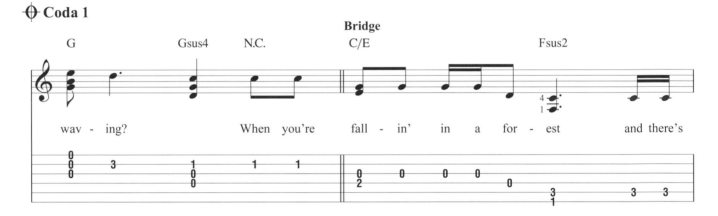

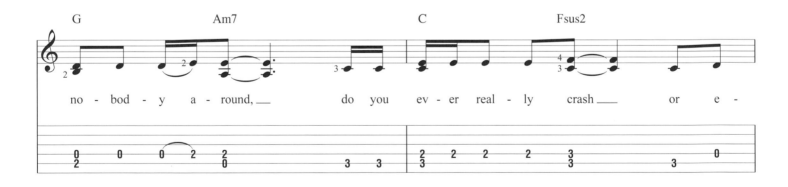

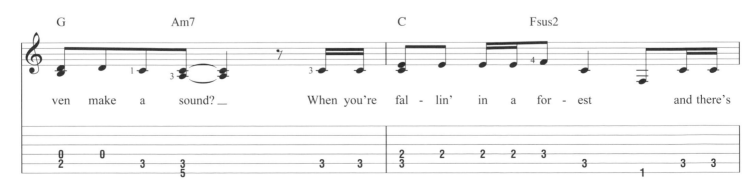

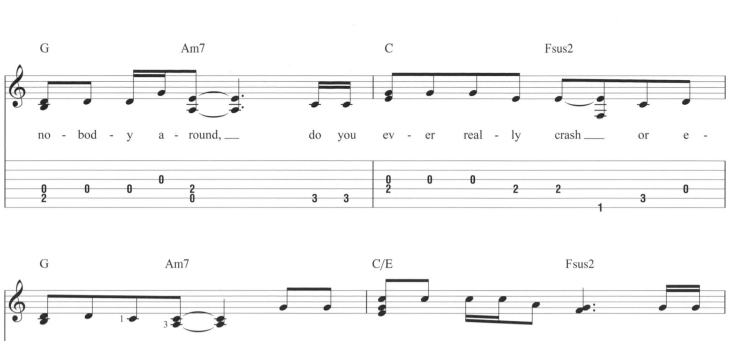

no - bod - y a - round, ___ do you ev - er real - ly crash ___ or e -

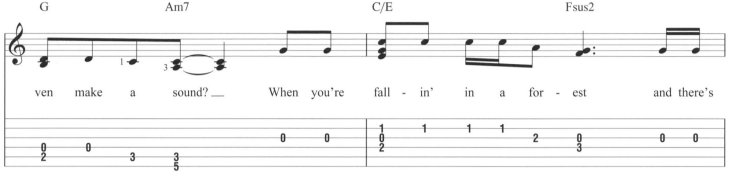

ven make a sound? ___ When you're fall - in' in a for - est and there's

no - bod - y a - round, ___ do you ev - er real - ly crash or e -

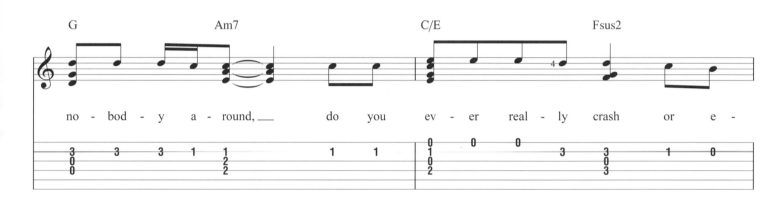

ven make a sound? ___ When you're fall - in' in a for - est and there's

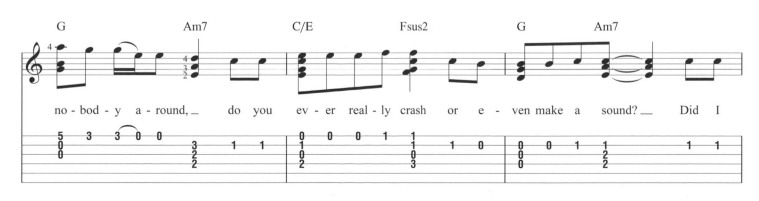

no - bod - y a - round, _ do you ev - er real - ly crash or e - ven make a sound? ___ Did I

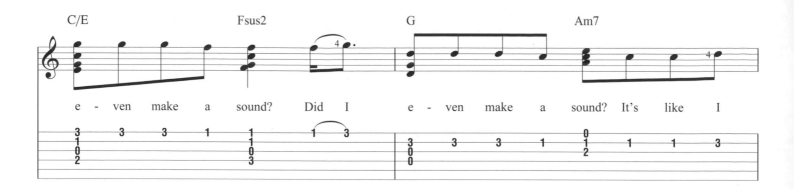

e - ven make a sound? Did I e - ven make a sound? It's like I

D.S.S. al Coda 2

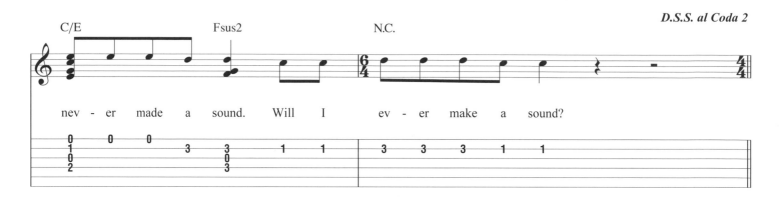

nev - er made a sound. Will I ev - er make a sound?

⊕ Coda 2

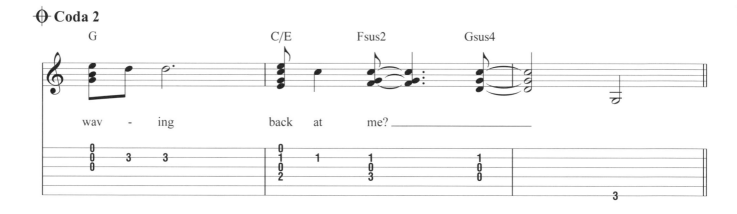

wav - ing back at me? _____

Outro

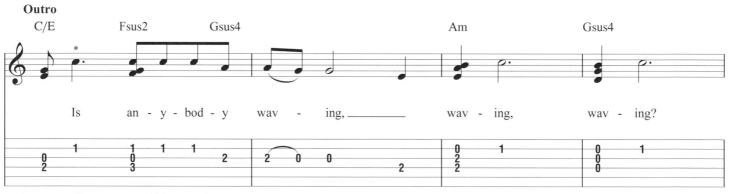

Is an - y - bod - y wav - ing, _____ wav - ing, wav - ing?

*Sung one octave higher, next 5 meas.

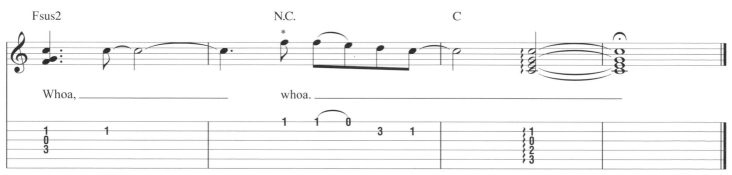

Whoa, _____ whoa. _____

*Sung as written.

EASY GUITAR WITH NOTES & TAB

This series features simplified arrangements with notes, tab, chord charts, and strum and pick patterns.

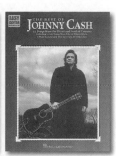

MIXED FOLIOS

00702287	Acoustic	$16.99
00702002	Acoustic Rock Hits for Easy Guitar	$15.99
00702166	All-Time Best Guitar Collection	$19.99
00702232	Best Acoustic Songs for Easy Guitar	$14.99
00119835	Best Children's Songs	$16.99
00702233	Best Hard Rock Songs	$15.99
00703055	The Big Book of Nursery Rhymes & Children's Songs	$16.99
00322179	The Big Easy Book of Classic Rock Guitar	$24.95
00698978	Big Christmas Collection	$17.99
00702394	Bluegrass Songs for Easy Guitar	$12.99
00289632	Bohemian Rhapsody	$17.99
00703387	Celtic Classics	$14.99
00224808	Chart Hits of 2016-2017	$14.99
00267383	Chart Hits of 2017-2018	$14.99
00702149	Children's Christian Songbook	$9.99
00702028	Christmas Classics	$8.99
00101779	Christmas Guitar	$14.99
00702185	Christmas Hits	$10.99
00702141	Classic Rock	$8.95
00159642	Classical Melodies	$12.99
00253933	Disney/Pixar's Coco	$16.99
00702203	CMT's 100 Greatest Country Songs	$29.99

00702283	The Contemporary Christian Collection	$16.99
00196954	Contemporary Disney	$16.99
00702239	Country Classics for Easy Guitar	$22.99
00702257	Easy Acoustic Guitar Songs	$14.99
00702280	Easy Guitar Tab White Pages	$29.99
00702041	Favorite Hymns for Easy Guitar	$10.99
00222701	Folk Pop Songs	$14.99
00140841	4-Chord Hymns for Guitar	$9.99
00702281	4 Chord Rock	$10.99
00126894	Frozen	$14.99
00702286	Glee	$16.99
00699374	Gospel Favorites	$16.99
00702160	The Great American Country Songbook	$16.99
00702050	Great Classical Themes for Easy Guitar	$8.99
00702116	Greatest Hymns for Guitar	$10.99
00275088	The Greatest Showman	$17.99
00148030	Halloween Guitar Songs	$14.99
00702273	Irish Songs	$12.99
00192503	Jazz Classics for Easy Guitar	$14.99
00702275	Jazz Favorites for Easy Guitar	$15.99
00702274	Jazz Standards for Easy Guitar	$16.99
00702162	Jumbo Easy Guitar Songbook	$19.99
00232285	La La Land	$16.99
00702258	Legends of Rock	$14.99
00702189	MTV's 100 Greatest Pop Songs	$24.95

00702272	1950s Rock	$15.99
00702271	1960s Rock	$15.99
00702270	1970s Rock	$16.99
00702269	1980s Rock	$15.99
00702268	1990s Rock	$19.99
00109725	Once	$14.99
00702187	Selections from O Brother Where Art Thou?	$17.99
00702178	100 Songs for Kids	$14.99
00702515	Pirates of the Caribbean	$14.99
00702125	Praise and Worship for Guitar	$10.99
00287930	Songs from A Star Is Born, The Greatest Showman, La La Land, and More Movie Musicals	$16.99
00702285	Southern Rock Hits	$12.99
00156420	Star Wars Music	$14.99
00121535	30 Easy Celtic Guitar Solos	$15.99
00702220	Today's Country Hits	$12.99
00121900	Today's Women of Pop & Rock	$14.99
00244654	Top Hits of 2017	$14.99
00283786	Top Hits of 2018	$14.99
00702294	Top Worship Hits	$15.99
00702255	VH1's 100 Greatest Hard Rock Songs	$27.99
00702175	VH1's 100 Greatest Songs of Rock and Roll	$24.99
00702253	Wicked	$12.99

ARTIST COLLECTIONS

00702267	AC/DC for Easy Guitar	$15.99
00702598	Adele for Easy Guitar	$15.99
00156221	Adele – 25	$16.99
00702040	Best of the Allman Brothers	$16.99
00702865	J.S. Bach for Easy Guitar	$14.99
00702169	Best of The Beach Boys	$12.99
00702292	The Beatles — 1	$19.99
00125796	Best of Chuck Berry	$15.99
00702201	The Essential Black Sabbath	$12.95
02501615	Zac Brown Band — The Foundation	$16.99
02501621	Zac Brown Band — You Get What You Give	$16.99
00702043	Best of Johnny Cash	$16.99
00702090	Eric Clapton's Best	$12.99
00702086	Eric Clapton — from the Album Unplugged	$15.99
00702202	The Essential Eric Clapton	$14.99
00702250	blink-182 — Greatest Hits	$15.99
00702053	Best of Patsy Cline	$15.99
00222697	Very Best of Coldplay – 2nd Edition	$14.99
00702229	The Very Best of Creedence Clearwater Revival	$15.99
00702145	Best of Jim Croce	$15.99
00702278	Crosby, Stills & Nash	$12.99
14042809	Bob Dylan	$14.99
00702276	Fleetwood Mac — Easy Guitar Collection	$14.99
00139462	The Very Best of Grateful Dead	$15.99
00702136	Best of Merle Haggard	$14.99
00702227	Jimi Hendrix — Smash Hits	$16.99
00702288	Best of Hillsong United	$12.99
00702236	Best of Antonio Carlos Jobim	$14.99
00702245	Elton John — Greatest Hits 1970–2002	$17.99

00129855	Jack Johnson	$16.99
00702204	Robert Johnson	$10.99
00702234	Selections from Toby Keith — 35 Biggest Hits	$12.95
00702003	Kiss	$12.99
00702216	Lynyrd Skynyrd	$15.99
00702182	The Essential Bob Marley	$14.99
00146081	Maroon 5	$14.99
00121925	Bruno Mars – Unorthodox Jukebox	$12.99
00702248	Paul McCartney — All the Best	$14.99
00702129	Songs of Sarah McLachlan	$12.95
00125484	The Best of MercyMe	$12.99
02501316	Metallica — Death Magnetic	$19.99
00702209	Steve Miller Band — Young Hearts (Greatest Hits)	$12.95
00124167	Jason Mraz	$15.99
00702096	Best of Nirvana	$15.99
00702211	The Offspring — Greatest Hits	$12.95
00138026	One Direction	$14.99
00702030	Best of Roy Orbison	$15.99
00702144	Best of Ozzy Osbourne	$14.99
00702279	Tom Petty	$12.99
00102911	Pink Floyd	$16.99
00702139	Elvis Country Favorites	$16.99
00702293	The Very Best of Prince	$15.99
00699415	Best of Queen for Guitar	$15.99
00109279	Best of R.E.M.	$14.99
00702208	Red Hot Chili Peppers — Greatest Hits	$15.99
00198960	The Rolling Stones	$16.99
00174793	The Very Best of Santana	$14.99
00702196	Best of Bob Seger	$12.95
00146046	Ed Sheeran	$14.99
00702252	Frank Sinatra — Nothing But the Best	$12.99

00702010	Best of Rod Stewart	$16.99
00702049	Best of George Strait	$14.99
00702259	Taylor Swift for Easy Guitar	$15.99
00254499	Taylor Swift – Easy Guitar Anthology	$19.99
00702260	Taylor Swift — Fearless	$14.99
00139727	Taylor Swift — 1989	$17.99
00115960	Taylor Swift — Red	$16.99
00253667	Taylor Swift — Reputation	$17.99
00702290	Taylor Swift — Speak Now	$16.99
00232849	Chris Tomlin Collection – 2nd Edition	$14.99
00702226	Chris Tomlin — See the Morning	$12.95
00148643	Train	$14.99
00702427	U2 — 18 Singles	$16.99
00702108	Best of Stevie Ray Vaughan	$16.99
00279005	The Who	$14.99
00702123	Best of Hank Williams	$14.99
00194548	Best of John Williams	$14.99
00702111	Stevie Wonder — Guitar Collection	$9.95
00702228	Neil Young — Greatest Hits	$15.99
00119133	Neil Young — Harvest	$14.99

Prices, contents and availability subject to change without notice.

Visit Hal Leonard online at **halleonard.com**

0819
306

easy GUITAR play along

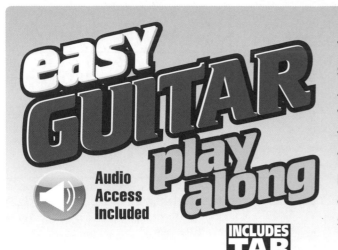

Audio Access Included

INCLUDES TAB

The *Easy Guitar Play Along®* series features streamlined transcriptions of your favorite songs. Just follow the tab, listen to the audio to hear how the guitar should sound, and then play along using the backing tracks. Playback tools are provided for slowing down the tempo without changing pitch and looping challenging parts. The melody and lyrics are included in the book so that you can sing or simply follow along.

1. ROCK CLASSICS
Jailbreak • Living After Midnight • Mississippi Queen • Rocks Off • Runnin' Down a Dream • Smoke on the Water • Strutter • Up Around the Bend.
00702560 Book/CD Pack....... $14.99

2. ACOUSTIC TOP HITS
About a Girl • I'm Yours • The Lazy Song • The Scientist • 21 Guns • Upside Down • What I Got • Wonderwall.
00702569 Book/CD Pack....... $14.99

3. ROCK HITS
All the Small Things • Best of You • Brain Stew (The Godzilla Remix) • Californication • Island in the Sun • Plush • Smells Like Teen Spirit • Use Somebody.
00702570 Book/CD Pack....... $14.99

4. ROCK 'N' ROLL
Blue Suede Shoes • I Get Around • I'm a Believer • Jailhouse Rock • Oh, Pretty Woman • Peggy Sue • Runaway • Wake Up Little Susie.
00702572 Book/CD Pack....... $14.99

6. CHRISTMAS SONGS
Have Yourself a Merry Little Christmas • A Holly Jolly Christmas • The Little Drummer Boy • Run Rudolph Run • Santa Claus Is Comin' to Town • Silver and Gold • Sleigh Ride • Winter Wonderland.
00101879 Book/CD Pack......... $14.99

7. BLUES SONGS FOR BEGINNERS
Come On (Part 1) • Double Trouble • Gangster of Love • I'm Ready • Let Me Love You Baby • Mary Had a Little Lamb • San-Ho-Zay • T-Bone Shuffle.
00103235 Book/Online Audio $14.99

8. ACOUSTIC SONGS FOR BEGINNERS
Barely Breathing • Drive • Everlong • Good Riddance (Time of Your Life) • Hallelujah • Hey There Delilah • Lake of Fire • Photograph.
00103240 Book/CD Pack $15.99

9. ROCK SONGS FOR BEGINNERS
Are You Gonna Be My Girl • Buddy Holly • Everybody Hurts • In Bloom • Otherside • The Rock Show • Santa Monica • When I Come Around.
00103255 Book/CD Pack.....$14.99

10. GREEN DAY
Basket Case • Boulevard of Broken Dreams • Good Riddance (Time of Your Life) • Holiday • Longview • 21 Guns • Wake Me up When September Ends • When I Come Around.
00122322 Book/CD Pack $14.99

11. NIRVANA
All Apologies • Come As You Are • Heart Shaped Box • Lake of Fire • Lithium • The Man Who Sold the World • Rape Me • Smells Like Teen Spirit.
00122325 Book/ Online Audio $14.99

13. AC/DC
Back in Black • Dirty Deeds Done Dirt Cheap • For Those About to Rock (We Salute You) • Hells Bells • Highway to Hell • Rock and Roll Ain't Noise Pollution • T.N.T. • You Shook Me All Night Long.
14042895 Book/ Online Audio........$16.99

14. JIMI HENDRIX – SMASH HITS
All Along the Watchtower • Can You See Me • Crosstown Traffic • Fire • Foxey Lady • Hey Joe • Manic Depression • Purple Haze • Red House • Remember • Stone Free • The Wind Cries Mary.
00130591 Book/ Online Audio........$24.99

HAL•LEONARD®
www.halleonard.com

Prices, contents, and availability subject to change without notice.

FIRST 50

The First 50 series steers new players in the right direction. These books contain easy to intermediate arrangements for must-know songs. Each arrangement is simple and streamlined, yet still captures the essence of the tune.

First 50 Blues Songs You Should Play on Guitar

All Your Love (I Miss Loving) • Bad to the Bone • Born Under a Bad Sign • Dust My Broom • Hoodoo Man Blues • I'm Your Hoochie Coochie Man • Killing Floor • Little Red Rooster • Love Struck Baby • Pride and Joy • Smoking Gun • Still Got the Blues • The Thrill Is Gone • Tuff Enuff • You Shook Me • and many more.

00235790 Guitar..........................**$14.99**

First 50 Christmas Carols You Should Play on Guitar

Angels We Have Heard on High • Away in a Manger • Coventry Carol • The First Noel • God Rest Ye Merry, Gentlemen • Good King Wenceslas • The Holly and the Ivy • Jingle Bells • O Christmas Tree • O Come, All Ye Faithful • Silent Night • The Twelve Days of Christmas • Up on the Housetop • We Wish You a Merry Christmas • What Child Is This? • and more.

00236224 Guitar..........................**$12.99**

First 50 Christmas Songs You Should Play on Guitar

All I Want for Christmas Is My Two Front Teeth • Blue Christmas • The Christmas Song (Chestnuts Roasting on an Open Fire) • Do You Want to Build a Snowman? • Feliz Navidad • Happy Xmas (War Is Over) • I'll Be Home for Christmas • Mary, Did You Know? • Rudolph the Red-Nosed Reindeer • Santa Baby • Silent Night • White Christmas • Winter Wonderland • and more.

00147009 Guitar..........................**$14.99**

First 50 Classical Pieces You Should Play on Guitar

This collection includes compositions by J.S. Bach, Augustin Barrios, Matteo Carcassi, Domenico Scarlatti, Fernando Sor, Francisco Tárrega, Robert de Visée, Antonio Vivaldi and many more.

00155414 Solo Guitar...............**$14.99**

First 50 Folk Songs You Should Play on Guitar

Amazing Grace • Down by the Riverside • Home on the Range • I've Been Working on the Railroad • Kumbaya • Man of Constant Sorrow • Nobody Knows the Trouble I've Seen • Oh! Susanna • She'll Be Comin' 'Round the Mountain • This Little Light of Mine • When the Saints Go Marching In • The Yellow Rose of Texas • and more.

00235868 Guitar..........................**$14.99**

First 50 Jazz Standards You Should Play on Guitar

All the Things You Are • Body and Soul • Don't Get Around Much Anymore • Fly Me to the Moon (In Other Words) • The Girl from Ipanema (Garota De Ipanema) • I Got Rhythm • Laura • Misty • Night and Day • Satin Doll • Summertime • When I Fall in Love • and more.

00198594 Solo Guitar...............**$14.99**

First 50 Rock Songs You Should Play on Electric Guitar

All Along the Watchtower • Beat It • Born to Be Wild • Brown Eyed Girl • Cocaine • Detroit Rock City • Hallelujah • (I Can't Get No) Satisfaction • Iron Man • Oh, Pretty Woman • Pride and Joy • Seven Nation Army • Should I Stay or Should I Go • Smells like Teen Spirit • Smoke on the Water • When I Come Around • Wild Thing • You Really Got Me • and more.

00131159 Guitar..........................**$14.99**

First 50 Songs You Should Fingerpick on Guitar

Annie's Song • Blackbird • The Boxer • Classical Gas • Dust in the Wind • Fire and Rain • Greensleeves • Hell Hound on My Trail • Is There Anybody Out There? • Julia • Puff the Magic Dragon • Road Trippin' • Shape of My Heart • Tears in Heaven • Time in a Bottle • Vincent (Starry Starry Night) • The Wind • and more.

00149269 Solo Guitar...............**$14.99**

First 50 Songs You Should Play on Acoustic Guitar

Against the Wind • Barely Breathing • Boulevard of Broken Dreams • Champagne Supernova • Crazy Little Thing Called Love • Every Rose Has Its Thorn • Fast Car • Free Fallin' • Ho Hey • I Won't Give Up • Layla • Let Her Go • Mean • One • Ring of Fire • Signs • Stairway to Heaven • Trouble • Wagon Wheel • Wish You Were Here • Yellow • Yesterday • and more.

00131209 Guitar..........................**$14.99**

First 50 Songs You Should Strum on Guitar

American Pie • Blowin' in the Wind • Daughter • Good Riddance (Time of Your Life) • Hey, Soul Sister • Home • I Will Wait • Losing My Religion • Mrs. Robinson • No Woman No Cry • Peaceful Easy Feeling • Rocky Mountain High • Sweet Caroline • Teardrops on My Guitar • Wonderful Tonight • You're Still the One • and more.

00148996 Guitar..........................**$14.99**

Prices, content and availability subject to change without notice.

www.halleonard.com